ANNE HOOPER'S

Intimate Sex GUIDE

*A therapist's guide to the
programs and techniques that will
enhance your relationship and
transform your life*

DK PUBLISHING, INC.
www.dk.com

A DK PUBLISHING BOOK
www.dk.com

Created and produced by
CARROLL & BROWN LIMITED
5 Lonsdale Road
Queenspark
London NW6 6RA

Art Editor Tracy Timson
Designer Philip Tarver
Editor Ian Wood
US Editor Laaren Brown

Creative Director Denise Brown
Editorial Director Amy Carroll

Photography Ranald Mackechnie
Illustration Howard Pemberton

First American Edition, 1997
6 8 10 9 7

Published in the United States by
DK Publishing Inc., 95 Madison Avenue
New York, New York 10016

Previously published in 1992 under the title
Anne Hooper's Ultimate Sex Book

Copyright © 1992, 1997
Dorling Kindersley Limited, London
Text copyright © 1992, 1997 Anne Hooper

ISBN 0-7894-2078-3

Reproduced by Colourscan, Singapore
Printed in Hong Kong by
Wing King Tong

CONTENTS

INTRODUCTION

Sex has often been referred to as the poor person's pastime — a reference to the fact you don't need to buy anything in order to do it or to enjoy it. We carry within ourselves all the ingredients for ecstasy, and even if we don't have a partner, it is still possible for us to enjoy personally created scenarios of sexual pleasure. But if sex is such a natural resource, why should we bother with books such as this one? Why don't we all glide along in a continual stream of orgasmic rapture doing, quite simply, what comes naturally?

SEX IS AN ACQUIRED SKILL

We often don't make the most of our sexual capacities because our grasp of them is uncertain. Most of us learn about sex from family and friends and the courting examples of our contemporaries. On a wider level, we learn about sex through the media. And, in our bedrooms, we attempt to put into practice the ideas assimilated. Ideally, this happens spontaneously, reenacting playful antics.

Life, however, is not ideal. We may not, in our inhibited Western world, get enough information about sex or enough of the right information. Not everyone has enough power of imagination to use sexual knowledge. Nor will instinct alone guide a person to good sex. Virtually all who reach the heights of bliss do so by accident.

And even if we find we are capable of orgasm, it doesn't automatically entitle us to certified bliss. How often have you felt curiously flat after orgasm? As if there should somehow be more to it? There are never, of course, any guarantees we can reach sexual nirvana, but there are methods that get us close. So one purpose of this book is to provide you with a good start and to increase your satisfaction using, in human terms, all natural ingredients.

TOUCH AND SEXUALITY
Touch is the doorway to stimulation. Through touch we explore our own inner sensation and intimacy with others. As we mature we develop and refine that touch, and sensuality widens into sexuality. This growth is encouraged by curiosity — interest in novelty.

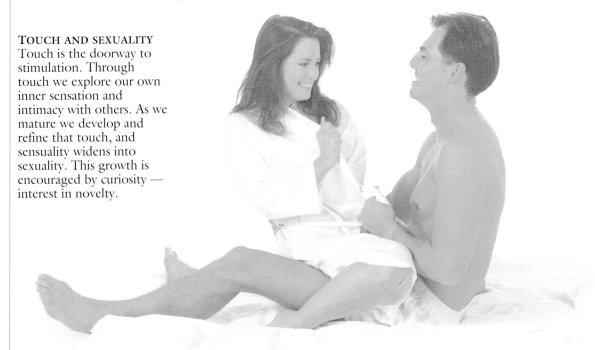

PROBLEMS WITH SEX CAN BE OVERCOME

Being unable to reach one's sexual potential can have long-lasting effects, not only on personal well-being and health but, almost inevitably, on relationships that are the most vital to us. Today, when people seek quality in all aspects of their lives, sexual fulfillment is an area that cannot be overlooked.

Sexual difficulties beset all of us from time to time and, if ignored, can ruin what would otherwise be a major source of satisfaction. Sexual problems are not usually of a great magnitude; most men are not prevented by impotence from engaging in sex, and most women can overcome pain on intercourse. But often an enormous gap exists between what we imagine our sex lives can be and what we manage to achieve.

Sexual difficulties are not new — they've existed as long as people have been engaging in sexual activities — nor are they particularly unique. On the contrary, they are long-standing, clearly identifiable, and extremely prevalent. They are also "curable." Over the years, sexual therapists like me have perfected techniques to tackle the difficulties that clients relate to us day after day. This book contains the programs and practices that can do the greatest possible good. Now readers who can't afford the cost of therapy, or who feel reticent about discussing sexual matters, can, in the privacy of their own homes, discover the ways and means of achieving sexual experiences that live up to their expectations.

A NATURAL APPROACH TO SEX

While I cannot guarantee that on perusal of this book you will automatically experience Grade A ecstasy, I can guarantee that by trying some of the sex programs you will enjoy gorgeous sensuality. Who knows? These items of sex information, factored into your sex play, may trigger a very special erotic experience — one that truly feels like rapture. And it is all done by knowing how to stimulate the natural chemicals of the brain and body.

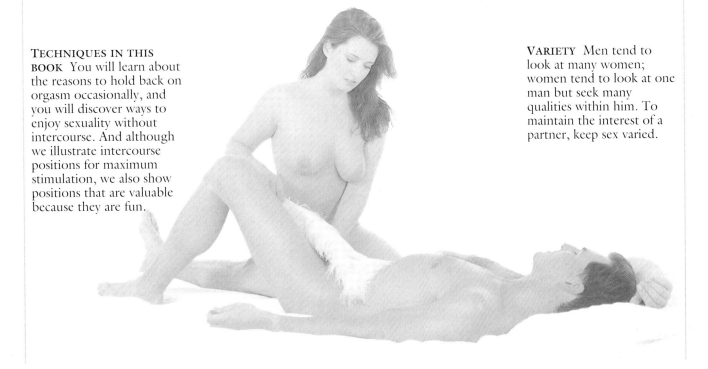

TECHNIQUES IN THIS BOOK You will learn about the reasons to hold back on orgasm occasionally, and you will discover ways to enjoy sexuality without intercourse. And although we illustrate intercourse positions for maximum stimulation, we also show positions that are valuable because they are fun.

VARIETY Men tend to look at many women; women tend to look at one man but seek many qualities within him. To maintain the interest of a partner, keep sex varied.

Few people realize that their bodies are a natural pharmacopeia. During sex we manufacture chemicals that make us feel wonderful. We produce an amazing substance that floods the tissues, allowing us to experience touch with dreamlike sensuality, and we also create, as a by-product of sexual climax, a substance that sends us to sleep, a pleasant, natural relaxant. And parts of the sexual response cycle utilize adrenaline surges, resulting in powerful bursts of energy. These allow us to take great satisfaction from sustained movement of the body, the naturally aerobic spin-off of the sex act.

In addition, our brains are able to send us on journeys into landscape and emotion without help from anything that acts on our bodies from the inside. We can gain other-worldly experience through guided fantasy or fantasy experiments that bring endless variation to sex and sharpen sexual sensation with concentrated intensity.

Children learn about themselves and how to become fully functional human beings through the medium of play, and adults find out about sex in similar fashion. Play isn't just the froth of life; it has purpose. It is a practical way of gaining knowledge and experience, not only of how things work but of how we work. Play is the building block of human experience. Playing, having fun, experimenting, literally fooling around, are all methods of learning about sensuality.

The programs and techniques shown in this book are based on play and on utilizing the natural resources of our sexuality. They have helped hundreds of people turn their insufficiently rewarding or boring sexual relationships into opportunities for uncovering new and exciting feelings in themselves and their partners. And the only necessary ingredients are imagination, erotic touch, and knowledge about our sexual selves.

THE ENDLESS VARIETY OF SEX

Often our sex lives stagnate because the sex act becomes boringly repetitive. The reason for this, ironically, is that when we hit on a good position (or a good combination of fingers and penis) we go back to it increasingly often. After all, we know it works. Yet life often remains interesting because of its uncertainties. Where Sigmund Freud reckoned that sexuality is our motivating life force and Alfred Adler said that a drive for integration is the explanation, I rate the need for survival a more realistic possibility. The drive to survive takes in both sexual urges and social fit, but depends most of all on what I have termed the anti-boredom factor — a drive toward stimulation.

Experimenting with different sex positions, or just looking at pictures of them in a book such as this, offers encouragement to those novelty-seeking brain cells. Indeed, it is by forgetting about the possibilities for sexual permutation that many relationships decline sexually. It's not good enough to explain that by knowing someone so intimately you automatically learn everything about them, and therefore there is nothing new to discover. There is always something new, but you must use your brain to find it. I hope this book is an aid to such sensual creation.

Even if only one basic sex position is favored, it can still be varied by the thoughts or dialogue you choose at the time. Physically, there are alterations to your posture or balance that may not seem especially different but, nevertheless, lead to other thoughts and feelings.

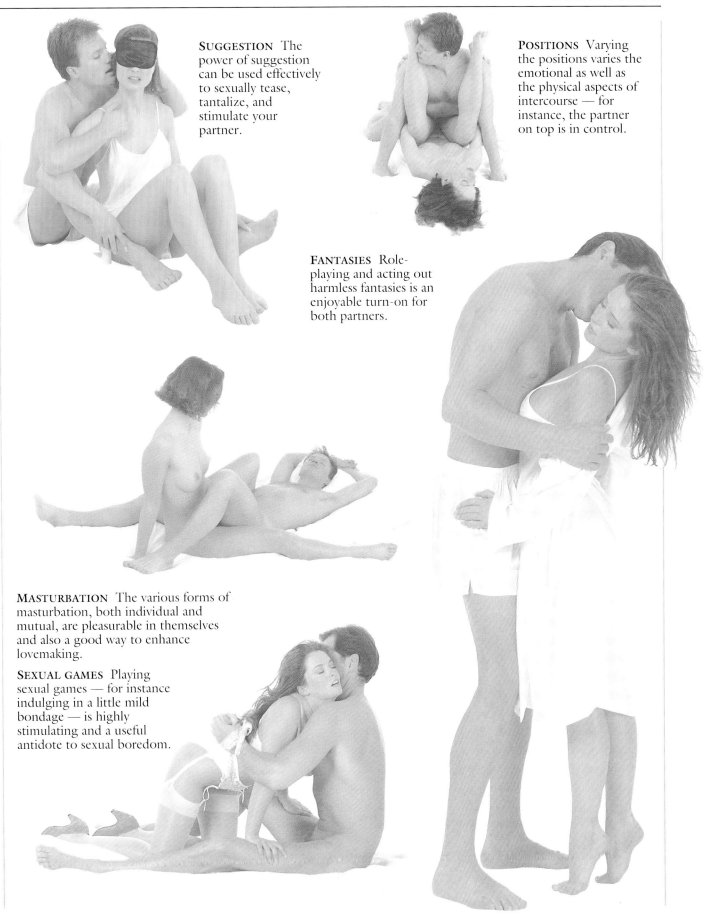

SUGGESTION The power of suggestion can be used effectively to sexually tease, tantalize, and stimulate your partner.

POSITIONS Varying the positions varies the emotional as well as the physical aspects of intercourse — for instance, the partner on top is in control.

FANTASIES Role-playing and acting out harmless fantasies is an enjoyable turn-on for both partners.

MASTURBATION The various forms of masturbation, both individual and mutual, are pleasurable in themselves and also a good way to enhance lovemaking.

SEXUAL GAMES Playing sexual games — for instance indulging in a little mild bondage — is highly stimulating and a useful antidote to sexual boredom.

THE ACT OF SEX

Becoming adept in the arts of sexual loving requires a clear understanding of the way sex works. Many of the difficulties partners face in their sexual activities can be caused by a lack of information about what happens during sex and, even more, how each partner responds and to what stimuli. Men and women share similarities of sexual response, but they see sex and attraction differently, and their needs don't always correspond. If taken as a process, the sex act has four distinct phases — arousal, penetration, climax, and resolution. Each phase may exist separately from the others, although at the best of times, the phases flow in a continuum. Unless we understand our readiness for and responses to each phase, our ability to have good sex — and sometimes any sex at all — will be seriously undermined.

AROUSAL

In order to want to have sex, a feeling of desire has to be experienced. Arousal appears to originate in the brain, though the phenomenon is still not completely understood, and hormones play an important part. When a man first experiences arousal his penis hardens and becomes erect; a woman's initial response is a moistening of her vagina. As desire increases with the exchange of a variety of caresses and the stimulation of erogenous areas, various other changes occur to both internal and external sexual organs. As desire reaches a peak, both partners long for penetration.

Fondling, stroking, and caressing each other's bodies produces sensations that will cause a man's penis to harden and a woman's vagina to moisten

Stimulation of the erogenous zones increases sensation. For a woman, kisses on the breasts and nipples are highly exciting; for a man, fondling the penis is greatly arousing

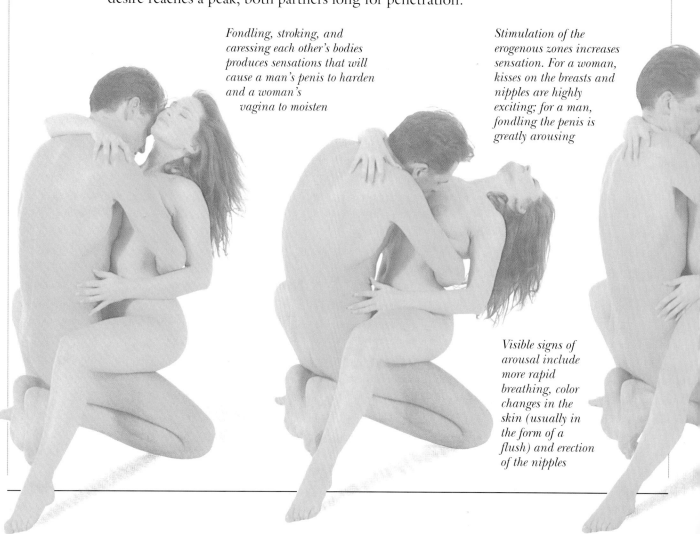

Visible signs of arousal include more rapid breathing, color changes in the skin (usually in the form of a flush) and erection of the nipples

PENETRATION

Foreplay should have prepared the vagina and penis sufficiently for penetration; the vagina must be lubricated by its secretions in order to receive a fully erect penis without discomfort. The vagina envelops the penis, and thrusting movements of the penis in this confined space produce sensations throughout both partners' bodies that lead to further internal and external changes, most particularly swelling of the genitals and muscular tensions. These, in turn, lead to feelings of such sexual excitement that, particularly for the man, a climax generally results.

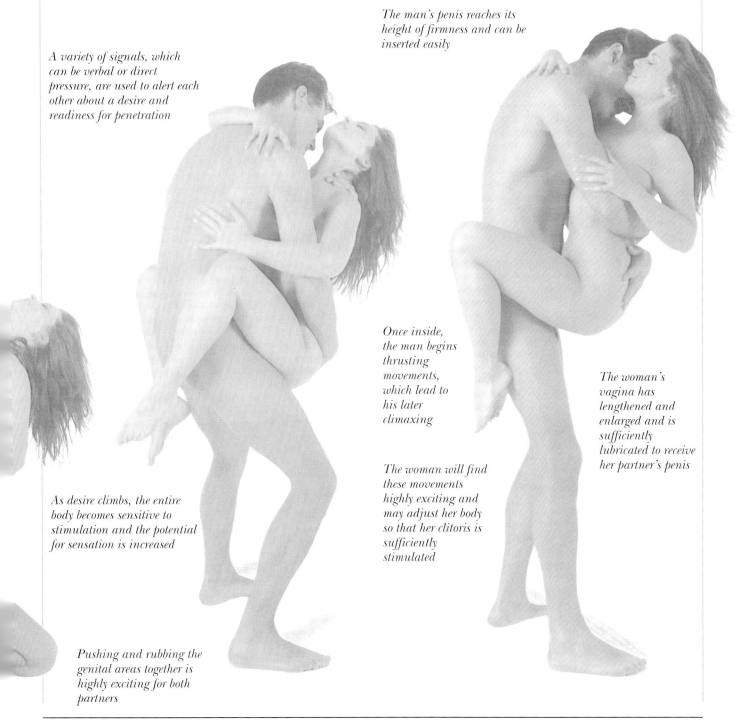

The man's penis reaches its height of firmness and can be inserted easily

A variety of signals, which can be verbal or direct pressure, are used to alert each other about a desire and readiness for penetration

Once inside, the man begins thrusting movements, which lead to his later climaxing

The woman's vagina has lengthened and enlarged and is sufficiently lubricated to receive her partner's penis

As desire climbs, the entire body becomes sensitive to stimulation and the potential for sensation is increased

The woman will find these movements highly exciting and may adjust her body so that her clitoris is sufficiently stimulated

Pushing and rubbing the genital areas together is highly exciting for both partners

ORGASM

When sensations become overwhelmingly intense, both partners experience a peak of pleasure which, with men, is almost inevitably accompanied by the ejaculation of seminal fluid. A man's orgasm depends almost entirely on having his penis stimulated manually, orally, or by the vaginal walls. A woman's orgasm, whether or not she achieves one, and how long it takes to do so, depends very much on the amount of stimulation her clitoris receives. This is a woman's primary organ of sensation. Again, stimulation can be manual or oral, direct or indirect, but direct clitoral stimulation brings the greatest and quickest response.

Rapid thrusts of the penis lead to regularly recurring contractions of the man's urethra and this, in turn, produces the highly pleasurable sensations associated with, though not dependent on, ejaculation. As the seminal fluid is spurted out through the engorged penis via the prostate and urethra, most men experience a powerful physical reaction. A man's orgasm is almost always preceded by a feeling of ejaculatory inevitability, and once he ejaculates, his orgasm cannot be delayed until emission has been completed.

As orgasm approaches, the man's pushing becomes more rhythmic and urgent, and his heart rate and breathing become more rapid

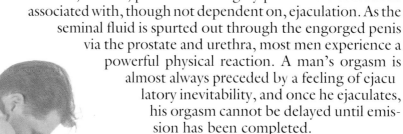

Just before the emission of the seminal fluid, the man passes the point of no return, when he can no longer delay climax

The woman's muscles contract and grip the man, and there is an increased blood supply to the vagina

A woman's pleasure proceeds in steplike fashion with that of her partner, her responses keeping time with his thrusting

At the moment of climax, intense sensual feelings flood the vaginal area and spread throughout the woman's body

During the most intense moments of lovemaking, the man's sensations are concentrated on being able to thrust deep inside his partner

Like her partner, a woman also experiences orgasmic contractions, similar in number and duration, and often at the same intervals. The sensation of orgasm may differ, however, from woman to woman, some experiencing a single peak of pleasure, others having more widespread sensations that can be rekindled, producing more than one orgasm.

RESOLUTION

Once climax occurs, sexual tension falls away. A man experiences an almost immediate drop in sensation; his penis becomes flaccid, and it will be some time before he can become erect again. This is known as the refractory period. After climax, a man normally feels relaxed and sleepy and often, depending on the circumstances, falls into a deep slumber.

For a woman, the return to normality is much slower. She experiences a slow and gradual decline in the swelling of her breasts and labia, and she remains in a responsive state for much longer, even welcoming further loving attentions from her partner.

It should be apparent, therefore, that although men and women are similar in their responses to sex, significant differences exist, particularly as regards arousal and the experience of orgasm. Often, too, we are in such a hurry for orgasm that we lose out on arousal. Yet it is the magic of this stage, that time when we are stimulated to a peak of sexual excitement, that helps the brain leap into a heightened consciousness. It is important that partners be aware of these differences and that they use the techniques shown in this book to give each other the best chance of a totally satisfying sexual life.

After climax, the man's sexual tension falls away rapidly; he soon loses his erection and feels relaxed and sleepy

The woman's sexual tension declines relatively slowly after climax, and because she remains sexually responsive she could be stimulated to further climaxes

Showing warmth and affection to each other will encourage a feeling of closeness that makes the lovemaking complete

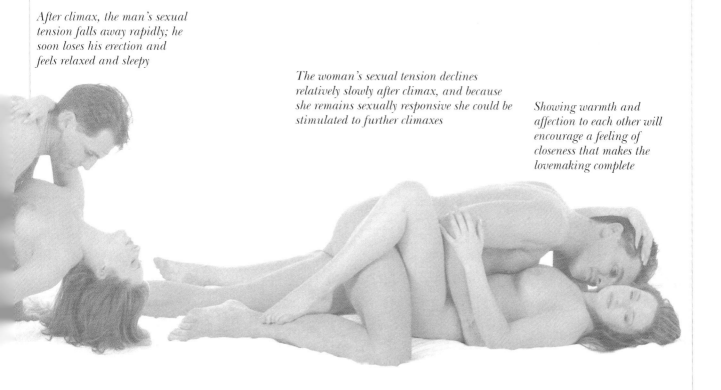

HOW THE BOOK WORKS

Many people believe that sexuality only has value if it is worked out in private, solely between the two people involved. This, however, is faulty reasoning. Sex therapy helps men and women to experience new thoughts and emotions as well as good physical sensations. Here, I offer assistance to all the thousands of people who choose not to meet a therapist face to face but who wish to resolve their sex problems. If you can make full use of the ideas, training methods, and therapeutic discussion I have gathered and developed over the years, I sincerely hope you will enhance your loving relationship in every way. The Intimate Sex Guide *has been compiled to provide you with all the information you need to enhance or improve any sexual relationship.*

THE CASE HISTORIES

Throughout this book personal case histories illustrate the sexual yearning and ambition every individual possesses but few care to admit to. The people whose problems I have concentrated on here encompass single men and women as well as those in short, long-term and/or conjugal relationships. The age range is wide, too. This reinforces the truth that disappointment with sexual experiences affects everyone at some time. These seemingly personal cases do in fact have implications for us all. I have tried in my assessments to generalize from particular circumstances so that anyone reading the case histories can pick up insights into aspects of their own behavior, and so perhaps be furnished with ways of adjusting that behavior.

THE PROGRAMS

Succeeding each case history are the therapy pages that deal with the problem being addressed; the pages include techniques involving specific mood training, factual information, and touch maneuvers.

The latter pages of this book help heighten imagination and show couples how to focus single-mindedly on expanding sensation and consciousness so that the brink of orgasm and orgasm itself become spiritual ecstasy. Each program is directed toward a particular aspect of sexuality, either mental or physical, and normally involves several stages. It is part of the philosophy and practice of sexual therapy that improvements happen over time and as the result of building on previous experiences.

ILLUSTRATED EXERCISES

Each program is made up of one or more exercises, which are illustrated methods of lovemaking. The captions and annotation guide you through the various stages and draw your attention to the finer points of the techniques.

These illustrated exercises are widely applicable to a variety of situations, and while you will get the most value from the book if you read through it completely you can, should you prefer to, work from it using only the exercises. I have personally seen hundreds of couples rekindle feelings of love while technically carrying out their sex therapy "homework" for me. The facts are that some people need help and instruction for sex and that therapists, like me, try to give it.

YOUR GUIDE TO BETTER SEX

On the simplest level, this book presents you with an enormous range of mental and physical practices that will expand your repertoire of lovemaking. One or more of the questions posed by the case histories may have a particular resonance for you and may provide a very specific answer. Do not be put off, however, if the individual circumstances do not exactly mirror yours, or if the recommended programs in their entirety may not, or cannot, be followed as outlined. They are there to illustrate the range of the possible, and even in isolation can help to liberate feelings and transform sexual behavior so that the sex act is enhanced and the relationship itself strengthened.

THE CASE HISTORIES, PROGRAMS, AND EXERCISES

HOW CAN I SHOW MY INTEREST IN SEX?

"For some people, meeting potential partners is easy, but developing the relationship is a problem. For others, the difficulty lies in meeting suitable partners in the first place."

A SEX THERAPIST deals with all aspects of relationships, even the initiation of them. Some people find their main problem with sex is a lack of it, caused by an inability to attract a partner or, having attracted one, being unable to keep them interested.

Men and women, as you can see from my case notes opposite, often have quite different hang-ups about their appearance and behavior that get in the way of successfully communicating their interests and desires. For example, many men erroneously believe that women are attracted by large penis size and a muscular body, while in fact, most women are repelled by these attributes but appreciate small but sexy buttocks, a flat stomach, long legs, and someone taller or of a similar size and build. And while men rate a woman's looks as the most important aspect of her attractiveness, different types of men are attracted to different types of figure and coloring.

Of course, physical attraction alone is not enough to sustain a close long-term relationship — there must also be an emotional and intellectual dimension. So someone who wants to find a new partner for a lasting relationship should pay attention not only to their physical appearance, but also to the way in which they behave and the impression of themselves that they convey to other people.

CASE STUDY *Steve & Caroline*

Finding a suitable partner and starting an intimate relationship is difficult for many people. For some, such as Steve, meeting potential partners is easy, but developing the relationship is a problem. For others, such as Caroline, the difficulty lies in meeting suitable partners in the first place.

Name:	STEVE
Age:	31
Marital status:	SEPARATED
Occupation:	ACCOUNTANT

Steve had recently separated from his wife after an eight-year marriage. Although he already possessed many of the physical characteristics that initially appeal to women – he was tall, well-built, and in good physical shape – he also projected an air of confident indifference that, in fact, obscured his shyness and relative sexual inexperience. He told me, "I find myself wanting to make love to attractive women but without too much success. Women usually appear to be interested in me when we first meet, but only occasionally do we manage to end up in bed together. Inevitably, however, it seems that somehow I do something to frighten them off very quickly.

"What do I have to do to not only get women into bed with me but to help my partners relax, so that we can have really great sex?"

Name:	CAROLINE
Age:	23
Marital status:	SINGLE
Occupation:	EDITOR

Caroline's one long relationship, which lasted about three years, had ended about a year before she came to see me. After it ended she had dated several men, none of whom interested her especially. She was a slim, quiet woman, with glasses, who was efficient and intelligent. She dressed in well-cut but discreet clothes and talked easily when addressed but did not volunteer information. She said, "I am impatient with the men who ask me out; most of them don't seem to have a brain. I rarely come across someone who is my intellectual equal. There is one man at the office whom I find attractive; unfortunately he hardly knows I'm alive.

"I know my upbringing holds me back from flirting, but I think that underneath I'm really a very sexy person. I have terrible hang-ups about my breasts because they're not very big, but I've got nice long legs and I feel I have a lot to offer the right man."

THERAPIST'S ASSESSMENT

What both Steve and Caroline needed to do was to project themselves in a sexier manner.

ATTRACTIVENESS
We all give off distinct impressions of ourselves, usually quite unconsciously, by the way we use body language and by our lifestyles and how we present ourselves. A zest for life, creativity, sexual interest, curiosity, and enjoyment are all extremely attractive. Steve's zest for life certainly wasn't apparent in initial conversations, and he only showed it when talking about his special interest in life — gymnastics.

Contrary to what Steve had originally believed, women are not initially attracted by outstanding looks and physique or even smooth talk. The surest way to become attractive to women is to treat them as alluring human beings rather than as convenient sex objects: no woman is the least bit interested in being just another notch on someone's bedpost.

Caroline was right to target her physical appearance, because this is what men are most attracted to. They respond far more to visual signals than women do, so the value of dressing seductively cannot be overestimated.

LOOKING FOR PARTNERS
My immediate recommendation, therefore, was for Steve to use his sports enthusiasms for breaking the social ice. His shyness would automatically be lifted, and gymnastics would allow his body language to reflect his more confident feelings about this aspect of his life.

I advised Caroline that she was going to need a partner who could deal with her intelligence instead of being intimidated by it, and that she must visit places where she was likely to come into contact with such individuals, perhaps putting herself in the path of men several years older than herself. She should display her figure more too, in particular her long, shapely legs, by wearing tighter-fitting clothes and shorter skirts.

Nor did she have to resort to flirting. Being able to gaze at someone and be genuinely interested in their personal story makes an excellent substitute, and providing information that forms a common ground and facilitates interest is a sensible move to make. Matching a potential partner's story with a similar one would show him that Caroline had emotions and a life experience similar to his, and would let him see that she was being open with him.

My program for
PROJECTING A SEXY IMAGE

Part of what is conventionally thought of as being "respectable" behavior lies in sober dress: if you want to seem discreet and unobtrusive, you dress quietly. The trouble with this is that, over the years, you can get used to the idea of yourself as quietly unattractive. However, the opposite is also true — gradually altering your appearance and your body language so that you experience yourself as an erotic individual can be a valuable method of overcoming inhibition. Once you have attracted someone with your appearance, you can use suggestive body language to reinforce the beginnings of sexual attraction, and then use touch to communicate your interest to your prospective partner.

Stage 1 PAY ATTENTION TO YOUR APPEARANCE

Becoming truly sensual is a result of internal changes that alter your attitude to sensuality, but these changes are easier to accommodate and can be speeded up if you tackle your outer sexuality first. Actually putting on a sexier expression as you gaze into a mirror allows you to feel sexier; altering your appearance slowly allows you time to get used to the change. Once you start noticing this change, other people will notice it too. The key to changing outward appearance is to take it gradually. Make one change every couple of weeks or so, and don't be afraid to experiment. And don't give up.

Stage 2 USE BODY LANGUAGE THAT IS SUGGESTIVE

Watch yourself the next time you meet someone new. The odds are that your arms will be folded, or your hands clasped in front of you. If seated, you may have swiveled sideways to avoid directly facing your acquaintance. If you are anxious, one leg may be draped over the other, maybe even wrapped around it. Or you may be huddled back in a corner looking as though you are trying to get as far away from people as possible.

BARRIER SIGNALS All these postures are barrier signals indicating that you feel tense or nervous or even under attack. To the person you are with, they show that you don't welcome them and you don't want them to come near. And even though we don't usually analyze the body language of the person opposite, and may in fact be unaware of it on a conscious level, our subconscious still takes in the messages being given and makes us respond accordingly.

If you want to make someone feel welcome, you need to be open to them. Avoid barrier signals. If you are standing, put your arms at your sides. Keeping your shoulders back and leaning forward slightly can indicate that someone has all your attention but that

WARMTH MOVES

• Look longer than normal into a partner's eyes

• Move toward the other person somewhat more than you would normally

• Smile more than usual, looking in turn at various parts of the body

• Nod your head in vigorous agreement

• Sit using open body signals

• When talking, use hand gestures that manage to take in the partner or that indicate an appreciation of him or her

• Take fast glances at the other person and while doing so, moisten your lips with your tongue, widening your eyes a little

• Make small touching movements. For example, when standing together, stand behind your partner cuddling lightly against his or her body, with both arms around the waist; put an arm around your partner; caress and massage your partner's back

you want them to notice you. If you know someone slightly, don't be afraid of hugging them or even casually resting an arm across their shoulders. These are displays of warmth.

If you are seated, resting your arms on the arms of the chair or extending your arms along the back of a sofa are indications that you are open to the person opposite. If you want them to feel in charge of the situation, ensure that they sit in a chair slightly higher than yours. If you want them to feel vulnerable, direct them to a chair lower than yours.

EYE CONTACT Part of a show of personal interest is an intent gaze focused on your partner's eyes. This makes the person feel special since research has shown that sexual interest is demonstrated by enlargement of the pupils and that this, in itself, is arousing. Men and women, judging photographs where one of a pair has had the pupils of the eyes enlarged by retouching, always rated that picture as the more attractive. (But don't overdo the gazing, or you will just look silly.)

EMULATION Body language can be used to emulate that of a person you are talking to, and reinforces the sense of matching. When a person shifts position, you can copy that shift. Once tuned in to the other person's body movements you can start altering your own, slowly, so that your body becomes open and receptive. The object of your attentions is likely to copy you unconsciously and assimilate the new feeling of intimacy this creates.

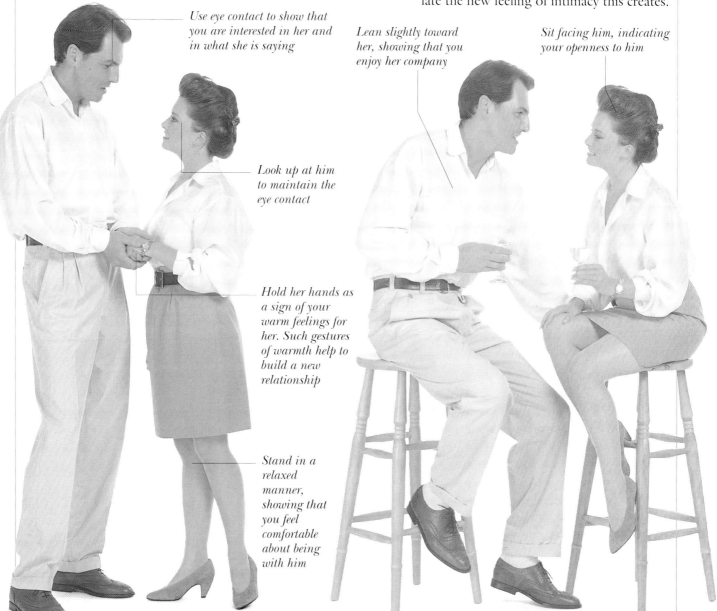

Use eye contact to show that you are interested in her and in what she is saying

Look up at him to maintain the eye contact

Hold her hands as a sign of your warm feelings for her. Such gestures of warmth help to build a new relationship

Stand in a relaxed manner, showing that you feel comfortable about being with him

Lean slightly toward her, showing that you enjoy her company

Sit facing him, indicating your openness to him

Stage 3 USE TOUCH TO SUGGEST INTIMACY

There are a number of occasions and opportunities when you can indulge in deliberate touches that charge your meetings with eroticism. It is important, though, that you deliberately hold back for a while from anything overtly sexual so that you lay the groundwork for a buildup of sexual tension: a mild withdrawal can seem tantalizingly provoking. Because your behavior will create mild anxiety, your partner's entire arousal level will be raised, thus readying him or her to be erotically receptive.

CONVEY WARMTH Hold hands on introduction a little longer than necessary. Look directly into your friend's eyes while talking, but don't stare at them. Use touch to convey warmth; for example, when you feel good about something give him or her a hug. If you feel concerned about something that the other is worried about, display your sympathy by covering his or her hand with yours. When walking, demonstrate your concern for that person's well-being by slipping your hand under his or her arm.

If you accompany a friend to a party or dance where you are standing together much of the time, stand close. When you are in crowds, put a protective arm around him or her.

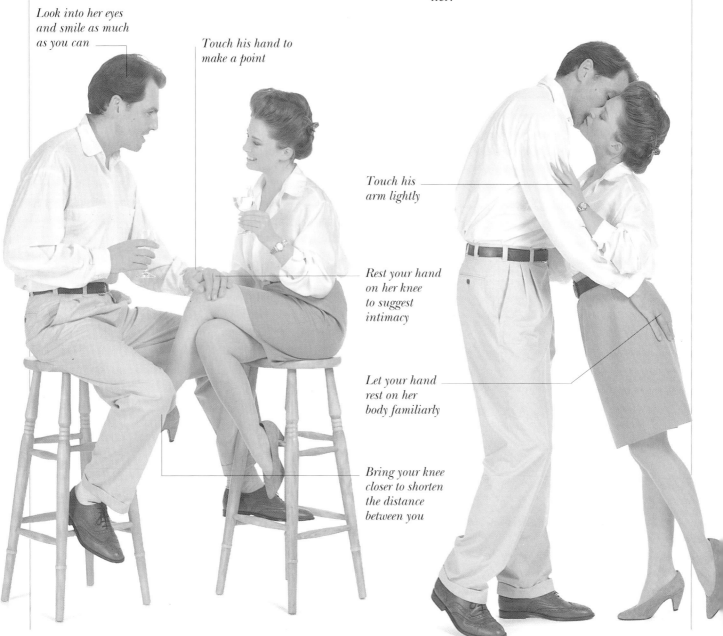

Look into her eyes and smile as much as you can

Touch his hand to make a point

Touch his arm lightly

Rest your hand on her knee to suggest intimacy

Let your hand rest on her body familiarly

Bring your knee closer to shorten the distance between you

INTRIGUING TOUCH As you get to know each other more, put an arm around your partner as you walk, and instead of resting a hand on his or her waist, place it farther down the side of the hip. If your hand reaches around near the pubis, even though this is still a casual touch, it begins to feel suggestive to the person experiencing it. But because they don't know whether or not you mean it suggestively, it also becomes intriguing. A variation on this move is to rest your hand on your partner's waist, and then let it slip a little lower so that it is on the small of the back or even resting on the top of the buttocks.

KISSING Kiss as a greeting: kiss your partner lightly at first, but as time goes by and you get to know each other better, make the kiss more direct and more lingering. Don't oblit-

erate your partner with the first kiss; make it light and exploratory, rather than fevered and oppressive. This may sound like very basic advice, but by following it you are setting the scene for truly sensual lovemaking.

By creating unhurried but sensual beginnings, in which your partner receives a sense of choice without feeling pressured, you are creating important foundations upon which to build a happy and successful sexual relationship. And when you get to know your partner better, and you begin to spend more time alone together, you will find that you have many opportunities to make everyday situations more sensual by the use of erotic touch. This will build up the sense of intimacy between you and deepen the feelings you have for each other.

Sensual erotic touch p20

IMPROVING YOUR APPEARANCE

POINTERS FOR MEN

• FACIAL APPEARANCE If you have a beard, consider altering the shape of it to allow your more sensual facial features, such as your lips and cheekbones, to show through more clearly. Your hair should, of course, be clean and neat, but it may also benefit from trimming or even a total restyling, preferably by a good hairdresser.

• GLASSES If you wear glasses, are they as flattering to your facial shape as possible? If not, invest in some that are — the range of frame shapes and colors now available means that practically everyone can find a style that suits them. Or consider a change to contact lenses.

• UNDERWEAR Many women prefer the appearance of boxer shorts to that of briefs, but whatever your personal preference is, the important thing is that they should be clean and a good fit. Old-fashioned cotton undershirts may be practical, but the new colored underwear that clings suggestively to the form is sexier.

• CLOTHES Stylish casual clothes, starting with basic jackets and trousers, can slowly be acquired to replace old drab garments. Beware of bright colors, if you wouldn't normally wear them, but concentrate your attention on the style and cut of your clothes: for example, blouson-style jackets team well with classic jeans or with casual trousers. If you are plump, beware of buying trousers that are pleated in front. Trousers with straight panels at the waist invariably look slim and sexy.

POINTERS FOR WOMEN

• FACIAL APPEARANCE Emphasize your facial features to bring out the best in them — outline your eyes and lips to accentuate them, and highlight your cheek contours with blusher. Pay attention to your hair; have it cut or restyled if it doesn't become you the way it is, and if it is a dull color, brighten or tint it. Don't forget to adapt the shades of your makeup to match your new hair tones.

• GLASSES If you wear glasses, are they as flattering to your facial shape as possible? If they are not, invest in some with frames that are a better shape or color, or consider a change to contact lenses.

• UNDERWEAR Throw away old-fashioned, boring underwear and invest in lacy briefs, bras, and teddies — knowing that you are wearing sexy underwear, and the sensation of it against your skin, will make you feel sexier and more self-confident. Wear discreetly patterned hose that show off the shape of your legs, and alternate these with lacy garter belts and sheer stockings.

• SHOES Start buying shoes with higher heels than you normally wear.

• CLOTHES Invest in dresses, skirts, and pants that cling and are made of sensual materials. Focus gradually on showing off the shape of your body.

• SCENT When you take a shower or bath, use body lotions and spend time selecting a light but fragrant perfume that enhances your natural scents.

SENSUAL EROTIC TOUCH

A variety of situations, including casual everyday experiences, can become more sensual and erotic by the use of deliberate touch. Close body contact and gentle movements will not only relax your partner, but make him or her aware of your presence at a level deeper than conscious sensation.

BRUSH YOUR PARTNER'S HAIR Brush away from the forehead toward the back of the head, first with your fingertips and then with a hairbrush.

Use a bristle hairbrush to stimulate the scalp, taking care not to pull or tangle the hair

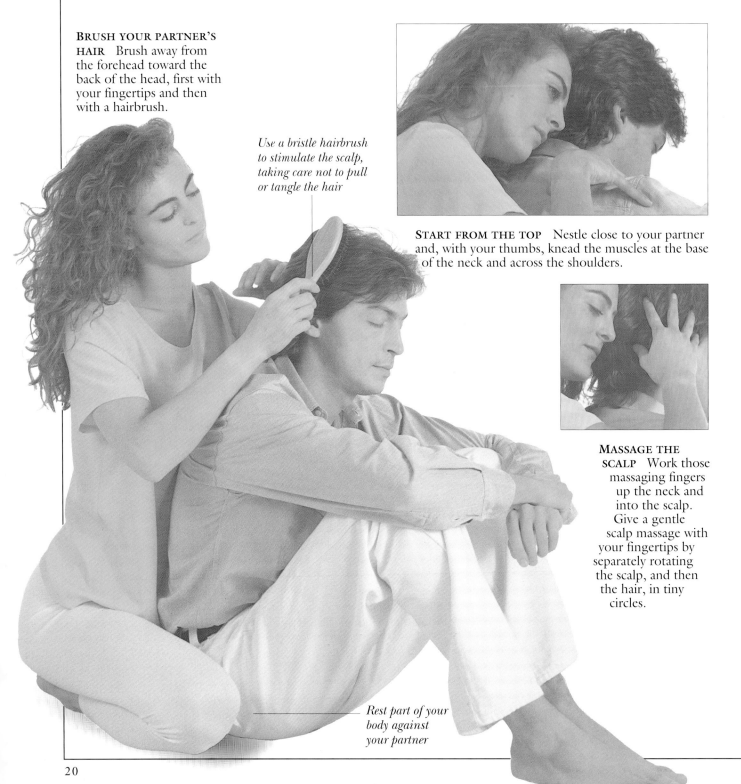

START FROM THE TOP Nestle close to your partner and, with your thumbs, knead the muscles at the base of the neck and across the shoulders.

MASSAGE THE SCALP Work those massaging fingers up the neck and into the scalp. Give a gentle scalp massage with your fingertips by separately rotating the scalp, and then the hair, in tiny circles.

Rest part of your body against your partner

TRAIL YOUR NAILS ALONG THE ARMS Lightly draw your fingernails from the crook of the elbow down to the wrist. Repeat this several times in different areas of the inner arms.

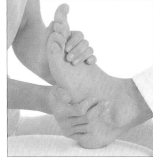

MASSAGE THE SOLES With both hands, and with thumb and forefinger, then your whole hand, massage the sole of each foot with a circling movement.

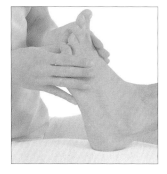

WORK ON THE TOES Gently push a slippery forefinger in and out between each of your partner's toes, turning it from side to side.

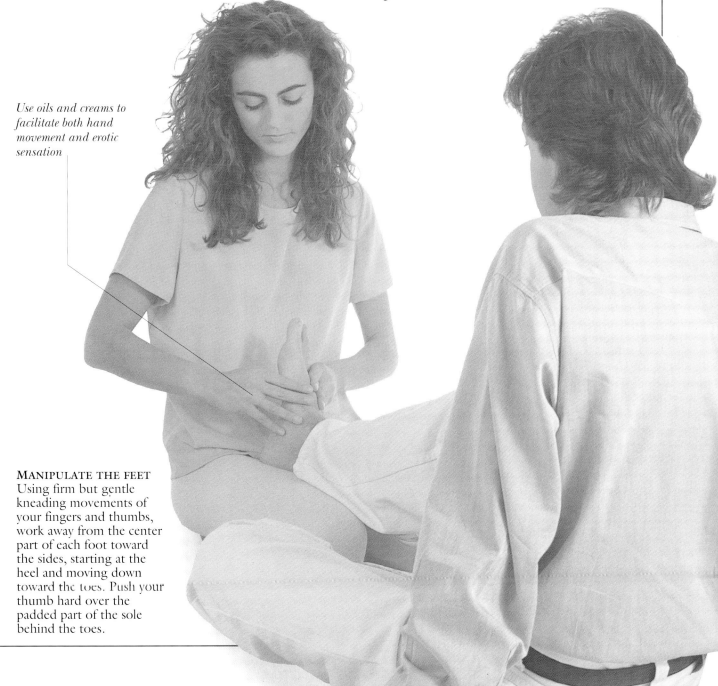

Use oils and creams to facilitate both hand movement and erotic sensation

MANIPULATE THE FEET Using firm but gentle kneading movements of your fingers and thumbs, work away from the center part of each foot toward the sides, starting at the heel and moving down toward the toes. Push your thumb hard over the padded part of the sole behind the toes.

BASIC LOVEMAKING POSITIONS

There are many different positions in which you can make love, and these simple and straightforward ones are generally recommended when starting a new relationship. They offer opportunities for intimacy as well as satisfying each partner's need to take control. However, because it is possible to make love in so many ways, trying new positions can be fun and will help keep your lovemaking from settling into a predictable routine — which can lead to the boredom that often destroys relationships.

THE MISSIONARY POSITION   The missionary is so called because, allegedly, missionaries sent out to "civilize" the colonies of the old European empires thought that it was the only respectable position for decent people, and insisted that their new converts use it when making love. Despite its staid image, however, it is an enjoyable position with many variations.

You should support your weight on one or both of your hands or elbows to make the most of this position

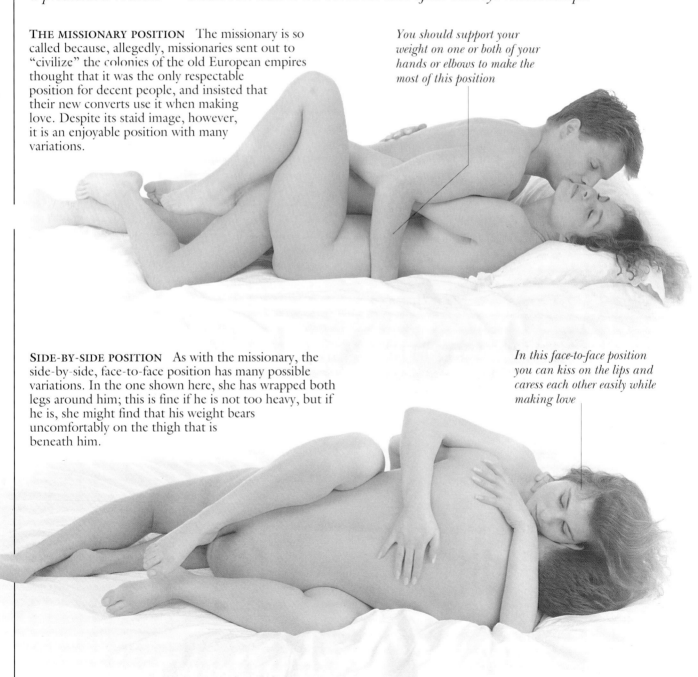

SIDE-BY-SIDE POSITION   As with the missionary, the side-by-side, face-to-face position has many possible variations. In the one shown here, she has wrapped both legs around him; this is fine if he is not too heavy, but if he is, she might find that his weight bears uncomfortably on the thigh that is beneath him.

In this face-to-face position you can kiss on the lips and caress each other easily while making love

You can use your fingers and hands to stroke and stimulate your partner's genitals and other erogenous zones

THE SPOONS POSITION   The spoons is a rear-entry position in which the couple snuggles up together, forming a shape said to be like a pair of spoons nestled together. Pleasant variations on this position include her pushing one leg back between his after penetration; him leaning backward away from her; and her bending forward from the waist. The last two variations usually allow greater penetration.

REAR ENTRY   There are many rear-entry positions besides the spoons and its variations. These include the well-known kneeling (or "doggy") position shown here, as well as standing, lying, and sitting positions, and those where she sits astride and facing away from him.

When you are on top, you can control the movements and the depth of penetration

WOMAN ON TOP   There are many different woman-on-top variations. For instance, she can kneel astride him and then sit upright; lean forward or lean backward; she can lie on top of him with her legs outside his or between them; or he can sit up with her on his lap.

SELF-STIMULATION When the woman is on top she can use her fingers on her clitoris to give herself greater stimulation.

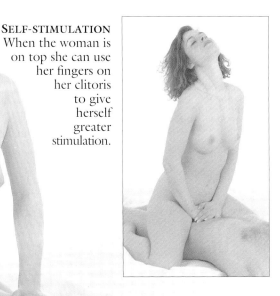

As well as being able to stimulate yourself, you can use your hands to give your partner extra stimulation too

HOW CAN I FULLY AROUSE MY PARTNER?

"Since good sex was always supposed to be spontaneous, it has been unacceptable to consider the idea of planning. And yet, if we truly want to increase our sexual options, that's what we need to do."

HOWEVER DIFFICULT a relationship may have been, men and women grow accustomed to the pattern of certain activities. Lovemaking is a prime example. It is possible to have sex with a husband or wife, year in and year out, with very little love involved, and yet the mechanics of the sex act will work perfectly.

Take away the feeling of familiarity, substitute a new partner, and a load of insecurities rear their insinuating heads in the subconscious. Sometimes it simply feels wrong to be making love to another, however irrational you know that feeling to be. Sometimes it is the pattern of lovemaking itself that traps you. Only the old one will work, but the partner who provided it is no longer in your life.

Sometimes the problem is one of trust; you can't fully trust somebody until they have fulfilled certain psychological criteria. Within lovemaking you may need to feel that a person cares so much about you that your sex problems won't matter; that giving you the necessary time for lovemaking is not only not a bore but a positive joy; that it is the human being who really counts, not just the sex act he or she takes part in.

CASE STUDY *Kathryn & Martin*

Kathryn and Martin were both experienced lovers. Each of them knew exactly what they were doing when it came to lovemaking, but over the years Martin had grown so used to making love in a certain way that he found it difficult to climax when he made love with Kathryn.

Name:	KATHRYN
Age:	31
Marital status:	SINGLE
Occupation:	TEACHER

Kathryn was a 31-year-old teacher who had fallen in love with an older colleague after having had several lovers, including one long-term relationship of six years. She regarded herself as sexually experienced and felt surprised that she didn't know how to deal with the situation she found herself in.

"Martin is a very special man," she said. "He makes me feel beautiful, dynamic and sexy, but we have a problem in bed. Everything's fine for me. He's a fabulous, imaginative lover, knows exactly what to do and brings me to orgasm in just about any and every way imaginable. The trouble is, he only manages to climax with the greatest difficulty, and we can spend hours having intercourse before he can come. By the time we finish, I'm tired, sore, and — dare I say it — bored? Is there any way I could speed him up?"

Name:	MARTIN
Age:	50
Marital status:	SEPARATED
Occupation:	TEACHER

Martin had thick gray hair and an attractive, tanned face, but an air of fatigue. He had recently separated from his wife and revealed that there had been little sex in his marriage for many years. Kathryn was the first woman he had made love to, other than his wife, in twenty years.

"I didn't have a very active sex life during my marriage, but when we did get together I had no trouble at all in coming. Now, though, it's as if the sensation in my penis is blunted. When we start off I do feel very aroused, but turning her on takes time, and by the time she has climaxed my first impetus seems to have vanished. Of course, I've been used to lovemaking in a certain pattern with my wife, and I suppose not doing this is impeding me.

"Did my wife do anything differently from Kathryn? Well, yes, of course she did. One of the things I miss is that she used her hands on me a lot. For instance, she was quite rough with my penis."

THERAPIST'S ASSESSMENT

Both Kathryn and Martin were saying, independently of each other, that they wished the other would speed up a bit. Unfortunately for Kathryn, Martin was experiencing a period of readjustment after the end of his marriage, and he was finding it difficult to adjust to new lovemaking routines. Moreover, he, like many other older men, had difficulties with stimulation: it is perfectly common for men to need more stimulation as they grow older.

EXTRA STIMULATION
The extra stimulation that an older man often needs may take the form of additional visual stimulation, such as the use of blue movies or books, or it may involve physical stimulation such as very firm or vigorous handling of his genitals. Many a man likes attention paid to his penis and genitals by his partner's hand during intercourse, while others also need some anal and prostate gland stimulation in order to climax.

MUTUAL TRUST
Then, too, Martin and Kathryn may not have learned to trust one another sufficiently. Martin hadn't liked to suggest that he should go ahead and climax first during lovemaking, instead of taking time to stimulate Kathryn, because he felt it would prevent him from satisfying her. It hadn't occurred to him that Kathryn might not mind this, or that she might love him enough to tolerate a lack of satisfaction occasionally. Another thing that didn't occur to him was that even if he no longer had an erection, there are many enjoyable ways of satisfying a partner other than by intercourse.

SPEEDIER RESPONSE
Once all these new scenarios had been explored in counseling, Martin did allow more feeling to seep through into his consciousness and ultimately his penis. He managed to be upfront about the methods he preferred: like many men, he favored very rough handling of his penis, and once Kathryn understood this his response speeded up remarkably.

USING A VIBRATOR
Martin welcomed the suggestion of occasionally using a vibrator to give Kathryn an especially intense arousal. He liked the option this gave him, namely that if, on these occasions, she climaxed quickly, he could remain spontaneous with his early excitement.

My program for
INCREASING YOUR OPTIONS

Most of us enter into sexual relationships with little thought about what we want from them. One result is that often we don't end up doing what we want, nor do we get the sort of lover we really desire. Part of increasing your options is to know yourself, your own responses and those of your partner. And by slowly becoming more daring, either on your own or with a partner, you will gain more confidence, will become more assertive, will learn to cope with rejection better, and will go on to initiate sexual acts that you may have wanted to do but didn't have the confidence to suggest.

Stage   LEARN MORE ABOUT EACH OTHER

Deliberately exploring yourself and your partner is the first step in learning what sexual options may exist for you. Self-pleasuring that leads to self-knowledge is vital, as is learning your partner's erogenous zones. Only by widening your knowledge of yourself and your partner can you give yourself choices.

EROGENOUS ZONES When you explore your partner's erogenous zones, start with the obvious ones such as nipples and genitals, and try out different ways of stimulating them. Then ask your partner about other, more subtle erogenous zones, and find out how he or she likes them to be stimulated.

After you have explored the erogenous zones that your partner is aware of, look for others: most people have more erogenous zones than they ever imagined.

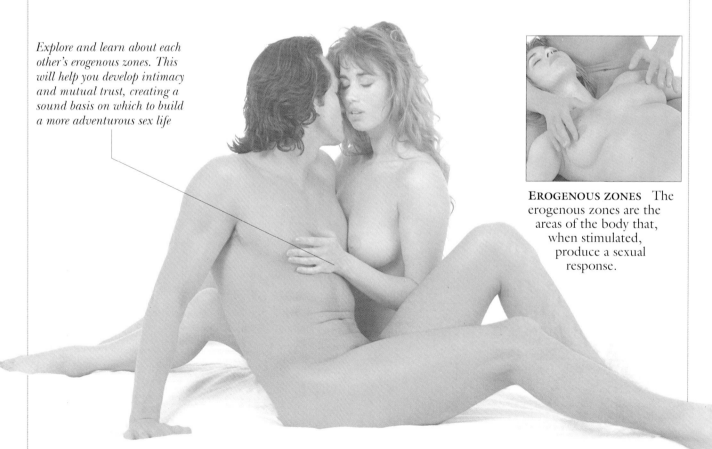

Explore and learn about each other's erogenous zones. This will help you develop intimacy and mutual trust, creating a sound basis on which to build a more adventurous sex life

EROGENOUS ZONES The erogenous zones are the areas of the body that, when stimulated, produce a sexual response.

Stage DISCOVER YOUR OPTIONS

There are a number of activities you can begin to experiment with to increase your sensuality and explore possibilities that may not have occurred to you before.

Sensual touch p20

STROKING Touching and stroking yourself and your partner are among the more obvious sources of sensual pleasure. Touch yourself slowly and sensuously after a hot bath, using sweet-smelling body lotions or oils and discovering your hidden erogenous zones. Stroke your partner from time to time, and in addition give "mental stroking" by regularly telling your partner, "I love you" and complementing him or her. Explain to your partner that you too would like to be touched and stroked, and share your feelings about this openly and freely.

MASTURBATION Learn to masturbate freely and with no guilt, and have sex only when you want to, not when you don't. Be choosy and seek the sort of sex experience that you desire, and don't be afraid to indulge in fantasy. Try expanding on your existing fantasies and bring in new ideas; if possible, find a fantasy that you can act out with your partner, remembering that you may have to adapt it slightly in order to cater to your partner's sexual preferences.

Be frank with your partner about what you would like to do, but be willing to drop the idea if your partner isn't enthusiastic about it, and consider any ideas and suggestions that your partner may have.

SEX WITHOUT INTERCOURSE Don't forget that there are plenty of non-intercourse sexual activities that you and your partner can share. These range from simply looking at and admiring each other's naked bodies to mutual masturbation and oral sex.

You can, of course, combine any or even all of these activities with intercourse. You might want to do this simply for the pleasure of it, or perhaps as a means of introducing an element of variety into your lovemaking so that you don't slip into a predictable routine that will inevitably become boring.

Either way, you will find that the sharing of non-intercourse sexual activities will add a new dimension of sensuality and intimacy to your relationship.

Stage ADD MORE OPTIONS

Even when you and your partner have learned to discover your options, there is still room for expanding what the two of you have found possible to do in bed so far. Taking what you have already discovered as your starting point, you will find it easy to build up a wide variety of loving sexual practices.

INCREASE EROTICISM Every day, tell your lover what you love about him or her, and also tell yourself what it is you love about you. Add to the eroticism of your lovemaking by putting mirrors alongside your bed, so that you and your partner can watch yourselves making love. An extension of this idea is to record the sounds of your lovemaking on tape, or even to set up a camcorder or a home movie camera and recorder and make a movie of it.

SHARE SENSUAL EXPERIENCES Masturbate in front of your lover, and try a new sex position every few weeks. When you have time, take a shower or bath together, then massage each other with scented oils and give each other a foot massage. Other shared sensual experiences you might like to try include brushing and washing each other's hair, eating dinner together in the nude, fingerpainting each other's bodies, reading erotica together or out loud to each other, and sharing a vibrator.

MENTAL EROTICISM Eroticism is, of course, a mental as well as a physical phenomenon, and there are plenty of ways in which you and your partner can show your love for and attraction to each other without physical contact. For instance, you could send each other love letters or leave love notes in unexpected places, or describe sexual fantasies to each other in explicit detail. You could even arrange to meet in a bar or at some other suitable venue and pick each other up.

SHEDDING INHIBITIONS Perhaps the main difficulty confronting people who are convinced that they are ineffective, and therefore couldn't carry out any of the suggestions mentioned above, is that of breaking away from their inhibitions. However, someone who is going through any experience of making overtures to a partner (or possible partner) is already making that essential breakthrough, even though they may not realize it.

SEXY UNDRESSING

Visual stimulation is extremely important to a man's arousal. A normal sex drive can be given an extra boost and a depressed one awakened by the sight of a female removing her clothes in a provocative way. A professional stripper will have had plenty of experience, and while no one expects you to be as good, you can improve your undressing technique enormously by regular practice in private in front of a full-length mirror.

Let a strap slip over your shoulder to hint at further disarray

Wear an underwire push-up bra to emphasize your breasts and cleavage

Rub your hand seductively up and down your thigh before removing your slip

Let some thigh show between the tops of your stockings and the bottom of your panties

SLIP OR CHEMISE   Your order of undressing, once the outer layers have been removed, might focus on your slip. One that you can drop and step out of, while still wearing your high heels, is preferable to one that is pulled off over your head.

HIGH HEELS   These are often a turn-on for men, because they make a woman's legs look longer and tend to push her buttocks to a sexier angle. (Try walking around the room in your underwear and heels, and see what effect it has on him.)

Keep hold of your slip as you step out of it, so that you can then throw it aside with the kind of dramatic gesture that a stripper would use

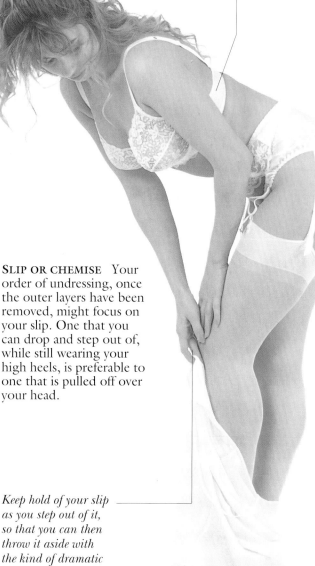

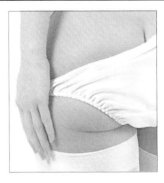

FEIGN MODESTY
Keep your eyes facing downward, feigning modesty. This false modesty will heighten his excitement by making him feel, subconsciously, that he shouldn't really be watching

PANTIES Pulling your panties off using only one hand looks more graceful than bending over and using both.

STOCKINGS AND GARTER BELT Stockings and garter belts are always sexier than pantyhose, and high-cut briefs or tap pants, preferably silk ones, are sexier than ordinary cotton panties.

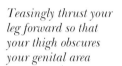

Teasingly thrust your leg forward so that your thigh obscures your genital area

STOCKING REMOVAL
Undoing garters allows you great opportunities for making delicious shapes with your legs, and slowly peeling the stocking away from a perfectly groomed limb is extremely erotic.

Adopt positions that you know are a turn-on

Use your fingers and hands to stroke your legs seductively as you slip your stockings off

TAKING YOUR BRA OFF
Being reluctant to disclose your breasts, and teasing a little about whether you really are going to take your upper garment away or not before finally daring to do so, will be far more erotic than if you just suddenly whip it off.

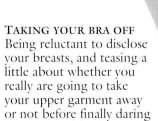

HOW CAN WE PROLONG THE SEXUAL EXPERI~ ENCE?

"Some men complain that they come too quickly, but when questioned they admit to lasting for more than half an hour. The question then has to be asked, too quickly for whom?"

EJACULATION control is one of the main causes of anxiety among men, particularly among younger men with relatively little sexual experience, and it is often coupled with a lack of self-confidence about sexual activities. Many men with a tendency to come too fast have anxious, overly tense natures. They may hurry through many ordinary aspects of their daily lives, their meals being a prime example.

But there are many different versions of rapid ejaculation, and ejaculation that occurs too soon for the couple concerned but is not, technically speaking, premature. Some men come too quickly with certain women, but have no problem at all with others. Such selective rapid ejaculation usually indicates something problematic about the relationship rather than about the sex act.

Also, some men come quickly when they are making love, but they can last for hours during solitary masturbation. This is probably because they do not feel that they are under pressure to perform when they are masturbating.

CASE STUDY *Alan & Maya*

Alan and Maya each had what they saw as a difficulty, and in combination these difficulties turned into a problem. The problem was not one of premature ejaculation on Alan's part, nor one of an inability of Maya to reach a climax. It was simply that Maya took longer to climax than Alan did.

Name:	ALAN
Age:	31
Marital status:	SINGLE
Occupation:	BANK CLERK

Alan was a bank clerk and meticulous but anxious by nature. He came from a divorced home and was needy for a steady partner. He had been dating since he was 14, and had had two steady girlfriends.

"I was really depressed after Annette, my last girlfriend, dumped me," he confessed. "But now I've met another woman. I think she's amazing, but I'm terrified I'm going to mess up this relationship too. One of the things that's on my mind, and this is because I think it was partly to blame for Annette breaking up with me, is that I'm worried I come too fast. It's not that I'm a premature ejaculator, I'm not, but my new girlfriend, Maya, takes a long time to reach orgasm. By the time she's there, either I've lost interest because I've had to keep going for so long, or I come before she's had her climax, even though we've been making love for half an hour. I really want this relationship to work. How can I get her more stimulated, and how can I hold out long enough to do this?"

Name:	MAYA
Age:	33
Marital status:	DIVORCED
Occupation:	BANK CLERK

Maya was Alan's colleague. She had had a number of boyfriends in the past, including a brief marriage, and was quite surprised to hear what Alan was saying.

"I hadn't realized he was so anxious about our lovemaking," she said. "He disguises it very well. But I've never been able to climax quickly. It's faster when I masturbate, of course, but I do wish I could find a man who somehow seemed to know what is right for me sexually. I think I'm asking for the impossible, though. I'm also aware that some of this has to do with trust. I do feel a great deal of trust in Alan. In fact, that's the reason I've managed to climax with him at all. I've had very good feelings about him. I have been able to open up to him. And the more I trust him, the easier it gets for me to climax, but if there is any way I can speed up my arousal then obviously I'd like to know about it."

THERAPIST'S ASSESSMENT

It's important to stress that needing to ejaculate after half an hour's lovemaking is not a sex problem, nor is climaxing only after about three-quarters of an hour's stimulation. But for this couple, the difference in timing constituted a relationship problem.

EJACULATION CONTROL
To improve his ejaculation control, I advised Alan to practice the squeeze technique with Maya. This technique is a method of learning to control the ejaculatory reflex. The woman masturbates her partner until he tells her that he is just about to ejaculate. At that point she squeezes his penis firmly, with her thumb on the frenulum and her fingers on top of the penis just below the glans, until his urge to ejaculate has gone. Then she continues to masturbate him, applying the squeeze each time he is about to ejaculate. By practicing the technique patiently and regularly, and trying to hold back without his partner needing to apply the squeeze, a man can learn how to control his urge to ejaculate.

STIMULATION
Alan also greeted Maya's statement that she didn't mind in the least if he came first with profound relief. How then to stimulate her after he had climaxed became an urgent concern. For the first time the couple talked about Maya's needs. "How is it different when you do it to yourself?" Alan asked. In subsequent lovemaking sessions he asked her to show him and to help him do the same. Although all this accelerated Maya's response, the couple needed encouragement since the improvement, on both sides, took time. At first it was easy to lose heart.

NON-GENITAL SEXUALITY
In addition to explaining ejaculation control and ways to give stimulation, I recommended that Alan should learn to focus on aspects of sexuality other than the purely genital. He then appreciated, almost for the first time, the touching, stroking, caressing, and cuddling side of sex. With Maya, he took turns doing the sexual enhancement program (see page 32). Besides giving him good sensual experience, it taught him to relax and enjoy pleasure which his anxious feelings had previously ruled out. Alan had, in effect, needed permission to enjoy lovemaking, and Maya too needed permission, in her case to use a vibrator (see page 90). This turned out to be something she had wanted to experiment with for years, but she hadn't allowed herself to do so.

My program for
SEXUAL ENHANCEMENT

Our mutual lovemaking routines tend to develop into certain especially rewarding patterns. There is every good reason for this, for the patterns we adopt are those that give us maximum pleasure, but meanwhile the alternative routes to sensuality fall by the wayside. This is a pity because, however marvelously a couple may embrace each other, it is always fun to have alternatives.

In addition to the benefits of having alternative routes to sensuality, it is stimulating to encounter feelings of newness; these are difficult to manage in a long-standing relationship. Regaining freshness in lovemaking involves using a sexual enhancement program that takes you back to basics, doing things together that you may not have done since the earliest days and developing a kind of touch therapy that restores your belief in each other and evokes delight. A good sexual enhancement program also helps to improve sexual communication by asking you to share your feelings and reactions with each other, and by encouraging a return to the days of petting.

Tactile eroticism p36

THE IMPORTANCE OF TOUCH Touch is possibly the most important and enhancing aspect of any relationship. Good touch takes us back to our earliest days when we were touched all over by the enclosure of our mothers' wombs, and to when, as little children, we found comfort and security in being cradled in our mothers' arms, and fun in playing touching and tickling games with our parents and our brothers and sisters. In later life, we in effect re-create these childish experiences with our lovers. But not all of us are good at touching, maybe because we received very little of it as babies, or because our partners are reluctant to be touched, or perhaps because we believe that touch is only acceptable when it is directly linked with sex.

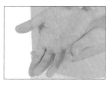

Erotic touch p20

BACK TO BASICS What follows here is a program designed to introduce you to the sensuality of the skin. It allows you and your partner to get back to basics and to rediscover hitherto forgotten delights by the use of massage and mutual caressing.

Stage I GIVE EACH OTHER A MASSAGE

Comfortable surroundings, privacy, warmth and a firm surface (preferably covered in a large, soft towel) to lie on are prerequisites for a successful massage session, as are warm hands and warm massage oil. When using the oil, rub it into your hands first before applying it to your partner's skin. Do *not* drop it directly onto your partner's skin because this often gives a distracting shock.

Your partner lies face down while you are giving this massage, which concentrates on the back, shoulders and buttocks. During your massage sessions, don't forget both to ask for and to give feedback. You are learning what feels good for each other, rediscovering forgotten sensations and creating new ones. Let each other know where touch feels especially delightful.

A general rule of massage is to make it *slow*, using the following basic massage strokes.

CIRCLING The first and most basic stroke, which can also be used to link other strokes, is to place the palms of your hands on your partner's shoulders and move them in circles. Move both hands in the same direction, working firmly outward and away from the backbone, and progressing down the back and along the sides of the body until you reach the buttocks.

Continue the circling on down the buttocks until you reach the upper part of your partner's legs, and then reverse the process and work your way back up the body again. The circling stroke can be used in this routine and in any other you want to invent. On the last circling session, finish below the buttocks. From there, you can carry out the next movement, which is the glide.

THE GLIDE The glide is the most spectacular part of any massage. Place your hands on the lowest part of your partner's bottom with the palms flat and the fingers pointing toward the head. Then, with the weight of your body directed from your solar plexus, start pushing both hands up along the spine, taking as long as you like. This is a heavy stroke, as you are actually leaning on your partner, who experiences it as a wave that flows along his or her back and threatens to engulf the head. After the glide, continue the massage by using swimming and thumb strokes.

SWIMMING The swimming action is similar to circling, but your hands circle close together in opposite directions instead of in the same direction, moving in the sort of way that they would if you were swimming using the breast stroke. You can do this stroke up and down all the fleshy parts of your partner's back, including the buttocks.

THUMB STROKES Working with both thumbs on your partner's lower back, make short, rapid, alternate strokes with each thumb, moving up the buttocks toward the waist. Carry this on up the right-hand side of the body to the shoulders, then repeat on the left-hand side. Finish off by concentrating again on the buttocks.

FEATHERING The light, skimming touch of feathering has a soothing and calming effect, and your partner will find that apart from relaxing the mind it enhances the effects of

SWIMMING The action of the swimming massage stroke involves moving your hands close together in opposite circles, much as you would if you were swimming the breast stroke. This stroke is best suited to massage of the back, especially the more fleshy areas of it, and the buttocks. As with all massage strokes, this one calls for the use of plenty of warm massage oil.

CIRCLING Circling is a basic stroke in which both hands move in circles in the same direction, unlike in the swimming stroke, where they move in opposite directions.

FEATHERING One of the most playful strokes for a massage is feathering. You skim your fingertips across your partner's skin, using both hands or just one hand at a time.

Give your massage on a bed or, if your bed is too soft, on a mattress, duvet, or folded blankets placed on the floor

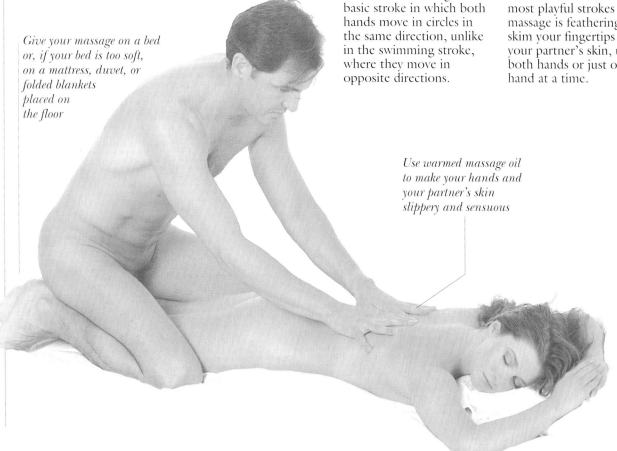

Use warmed massage oil to make your hands and your partner's skin slippery and sensuous

the whole massage session. It feels good after the firmer types of massage such as circling, kneading, and thumb strokes, and you can use it at any point (and any number of times) during your massage session. You can also use a variation of it at the start of the session, before you begin the circling, as a pleasurable and relaxing way of applying the warmed massage oil to your partner's body.

Begin by giving your partner a series of gentle, flowing hand strokes. Using the palm and fingers, draw your hand as lightly as possible down your partner's back from shoulders to buttocks. Just as your hand reaches your partner's buttocks and you are about to lift it away, begin a second stroke with your other hand.

Continue in this fashion for about a dozen such overlapping strokes, so that the sensation your partner feels is of one long, continuous stroke. Repeat the stroking down the back of each leg, and then repeat the back and leg strokes all over again, using only the tips of your fingers and touching your partner's skin as lightly as you can.

KNUCKLING You can apply firm, localized pressure to areas such as the shoulders, chest, hands, legs and feet by using your thumbs, either by simply pressing with them to apply static pressure for a few seconds or by moving them in small circles to create rippling, circular waves of pressure. An alternative to this thumb pressure is to use knuckling strokes.

PRESSURE Use your thumbs to exert localized pressure — either static pressure, when you press for a few seconds before moving to a new position, or circular pressure, in which you move your thumbs in small circles.

KNEADING The kneading massage stroke is, as its name implies, the sort of action you use when kneading dough. It is particularly useful for massaging the fleshier areas of your partner's body, such as the buttocks and thighs, and also for the shoulders and the base of the neck.

Always take your time when giving a massage — make your strokes slow and sensuous

KNUCKLING Use your knuckles to massage your partner's shoulders, chest, palms and soles. Use small, circular movements to create a rippling effect.

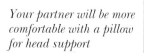

Your partner will be more comfortable with a pillow for head support

As the name suggests, this involves using your knuckles, moving them in small, circular strokes to create a rippling effect on your partner's skin and the underlying flesh.

Use the middle sections of your fingers for these strokes, with the fingers curled back so that their tips are lightly pressing against your palms. Like kneading, knuckling is especially suitable for massaging the upper chest, the shoulders and the base of the neck, and for the hands and feet and the tops and outer sides of the thighs.

To massage a hand by using knuckling, first support it palm-up in one of your own hands. Then work the knuckles of your other hand into the palm with small, circular movements, covering the whole palm and using pressure that varies from light to firm. Use this stroke in conjunction with thumb pressure — applied to the palm and to the back of the hand — to loosen up and relax the muscles and tendons. Use a similar combination of knuckles and thumb to massage your partner's feet.

KNEADING   Kneading is a massage stroke that employs the same sort of action as you would use when kneading dough— you take an area of flesh between your fingers and thumb and alternately squeeze and release it. Light kneading will stretch and relax the skin and the muscles that lie just beneath it; to massage the deeper muscles the kneading action must be firmer.

Kneading is especially useful for massaging and relaxing the fleshier parts of your partner's body, such as his or her buttocks, hips and thighs, and for dispelling the tension from the shoulders and the base of the neck. It can, however, be used on any part of the body where there is sufficient flesh to make the stroke effective and pleasurable.

The basic kneading action involves both hands, which you place flat on your partner's skin, side by side with thumbs extended sideways. Press the palm of one hand down so that a bulge of your partner's flesh is squeezed up into the area between your thumb and forefinger. Grasp the flesh with that hand and gently squeeze it, then as you release it grasp it with the other hand. Repeat this action several times, rhythmically squeezing and releasing the flesh with alternate hands.

When you become practiced at this stroke, you will be able to squeeze the flesh so that it appears to travel from one hand to the other with a short, wavelike motion. Use a firm, deep kneading action on particularly fleshy parts of the body such as the buttocks and the outer sides of the thighs and hips. To make the kneading action even more deep and stimulating when you are massaging these areas, give each handful of flesh a firm but gentle twisting motion in addition to the basic squeezing action.

Less fleshy areas (such as the inner thighs and the calves, abdomen, chest, back, shoulders, neck and arms) require a relatively light kneading.

Stage 2 — USE MASSAGE FOR SEXUAL ENHANCEMENT

Begin with a warm bath, preferably shared. Soap each other's body lingeringly, and let your slippery fingers glide around each other's curves. Lie back and luxuriate in the warmth, and enjoy the sensation of skin on skin. Take your time.

Once out of the bath, wrap each other in warm, fluffy towels, and move to a warm bedroom (all this heating-up needs to have been organized in advance). You are now going to take turns giving each other a massage, but you should agree not to have intercourse (this removes any performance demands), and for half an hour each of you massages the other. The one being massaged tells the other exactly how it feels to be touched in every part of the body — except the genitals, which you may not touch at this stage — and describes in turn how he or she would like to be touched. You are just trying to give and receive pleasure at this stage, and you should repeat this procedure at two or three one-hour sessions a week, at times when you are ensured privacy.

Stage 3 — GENITAL PLEASURING

Begin with the warm bath as before, and then move to the bedroom. Once again, you should agree not to have intercourse. Continue with  the massages, but this time include the genitals. The purpose of this is to provide information about response to touch and to give good sensual feeling. The man should explain how he likes to be touched on his penis

Sensual massage p56

and the woman how she likes to be touched on, at or near the vagina and clitoris. You should both be trying to give pleasure, but not trying to give orgasm.

TACTILE EROTICISM

Exploring the erotic delights of touching and being touched is not only great fun, it also encourages trust and intimacy and helps to develop good sexual communication between you and your partner. In addition, by making you more aware of your own responses to touch and by teaching you more about your partner's responses, it is a useful technique for enhancing or rejuvenating your sex life.

A TOUCH OF SILK Silk has long been prized for its sensual delicacy, and you can use it to stroke and tantalize your partner to great effect. Use a silk scarf or handkerchief, trailing one end of it lightly and teasingly across your partner's naked skin.

Draw the silk across her skin as slowly as possible to maximize the eroticism of the sensation

One effect of being blindfolded is a dramatic heightening of your sensitivity to touch

Use the hairbrush with one hand while stroking him gently with the other

BRUSH STROKES A completely different sensation from that provided by silk can be obtained by the gentle use of brushes. Use a soft-bristled brush, such as a baby's hairbrush, to tickle and stimulate your partner's bare skin (above), and a harder-bristled brush to groom your partner's hair and massage his or her scalp (left).

He will find that the tingling feeling created by the scalp massage is pleasantly relaxing and soothing

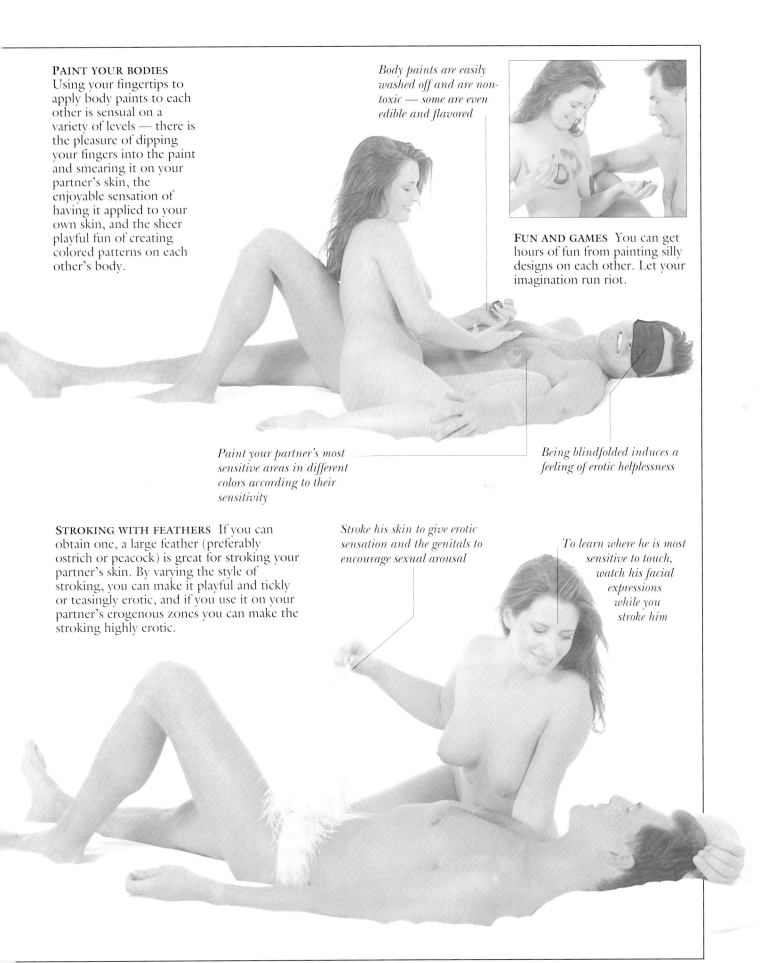

PAINT YOUR BODIES

Using your fingertips to apply body paints to each other is sensual on a variety of levels — there is the pleasure of dipping your fingers into the paint and smearing it on your partner's skin, the enjoyable sensation of having it applied to your own skin, and the sheer playful fun of creating colored patterns on each other's body.

Body paints are easily washed off and are non-toxic — some are even edible and flavored

FUN AND GAMES You can get hours of fun from painting silly designs on each other. Let your imagination run riot.

Paint your partner's most sensitive areas in different colors according to their sensitivity

Being blindfolded induces a feeling of erotic helplessness

STROKING WITH FEATHERS

STROKING WITH FEATHERS If you can obtain one, a large feather (preferably ostrich or peacock) is great for stroking your partner's skin. By varying the style of stroking, you can make it playful and tickly or teasingly erotic, and if you use it on your partner's erogenous zones you can make the stroking highly erotic.

Stroke his skin to give erotic sensation and the genitals to encourage sexual arousal

To learn where he is most sensitive to touch, watch his facial expressions while you stroke him

A SEXUAL BANQUET

Eating and making love are two of life's great sensual activities. The mouth, one of the most versatile parts of the body, is capable of giving and experiencing pleasure in a variety of ways. To create a sexual banquet, the kissing, sucking on, nibbling, and gentle biting of a lover's body can be imaginatively combined with the erotic application of specially selected foods to create an experience that is tasty in every sense. This touch of the exotic should help to widen sexual horizons in a most enjoyable way.

TREAT YOUR PARTNER
As a special sensual surprise — say when your partner has just emerged from a relaxing bath — prepare a dish of fruits and other delicious fare, and serve with some chilled wine.

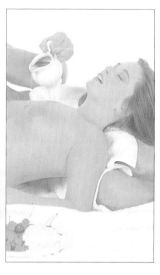

Make the experience more erotic by feeding your partner

Take turns offering food to each other

POUR ON THE PLEASURE
A little honey, syrup, or some champagne feels good going on over the breasts and navel.

Use bath towels to protect your sheets and bedding

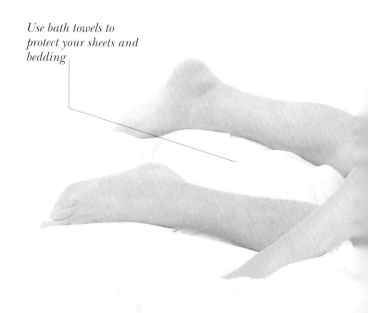

USE YOUR MOUTH CREATIVELY   Lick and suck up the honey, syrup, or wine from your partner's body, making exaggerated gestures with your tongue. Long sweeps of your tongue's rough surface will feel incredibly sensuous and are bound to make your partner feel good.

APPLY BODY "PAINT"
Cream can be dabbed onto your partner's nipples using slow circular movements, and can be sucked off afterward.

Let her know she looks good enough to eat

Move teasingly close to her genitals

STRATEGIC POSITIONING
Place some fruit close to your partner's genitals and eat it off him or her in a provocative way.

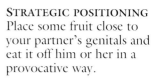

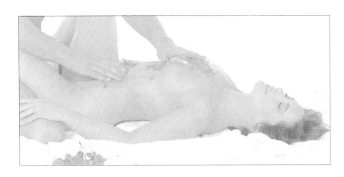

NO HOLDS BARRED Smear your partner all over with soft fruit, crushing it against his or her naked body and rubbing it slowly and sensuously up and down and around in circles (see left). You can even heighten the feelings of erotic intimacy by feeding each other mouth-to-mouth while continuing to caress each other through the fruit. When you are both thoroughly aroused and ready, bring your sexual banquet to a glorious climax by making love while continuing to massage each other with the crushed fruit (below).

Seductively press the fruit against your partner's body

Let your partner see how much you are enjoying this novel experience

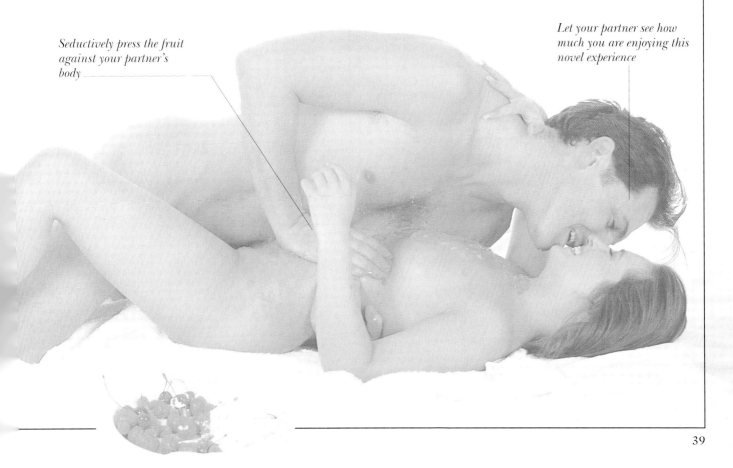

HOW CAN I MAKE LOVE~ MAKING MORE INTIMATE?

"Opening your innermost self to your partner can be difficult, but it is essential if you want your relationship to flourish and grow."

JUST BECAUSE two people make love does not, surprisingly enough, guarantee that they are intimate. Intimacy is a quality that grows through a sharing of feelings; it heightens all aspects of the relationship and is the main ingredient responsible for turning sex into an ecstatic experience as opposed to a pleasurable but uninspiring one.

In order to achieve intimacy we need to be brave enough to reveal our innermost selves to our partners, which is something that many people find difficult to do.

This difficulty may arise for many people because they worry that their inner selves might be unacceptable, or because they feel that revealing too much about themselves to another person (even though that person may be someone who is very close to them) will make them vulnerable in some way.

Creating the conditions in which your lover feels safe enough to talk about deep, inner feelings helps him or her to overcome such fears, and so does the ability to open up and share your own feelings.

CASE STUDY *Maria & Jack*

Although Maria and Jack had known each other only a short time, they got along very well together, both in bed and out of it. But they found it difficult to be truly intimate with each other and to confide their innermost thoughts and feelings, and that left them both dissatisfied.

Name:	MARIA
Age:	28
Marital status:	SINGLE
Occupation:	HAIRDRESSER

Maria was from an Italian-American family, and her brother, two sisters, and most of her cousins were already married. She had some strongly independent ideas about life, though, and owned her own car and house.

"I don't have any difficulty in attracting men," she said, "I'm dating an extremely interesting guy at the moment. He's ambitious and bright and I'm learning a lot from him. He'd be a suitable husband but, as happened with the last couple of boyfriends I had, I can't really be myself with him when we go to bed.

"It's not that I'm afraid of talking about sex or of making sexual suggestions, but there is a feeling, at the end of lovemaking, that things aren't quite right. I don't feel really relaxed, even though I've climaxed. Afterward, I feel a million miles away from him. I look at him and wonder what he's thinking. And because he never opens up to me, I don't really reveal my inner self to him. I'd like to. But I'm not quite sure how to."

Name:	JACK
Age:	37
Marital status:	SINGLE
Occupation:	TRANSPORT MANAGER

Jack was brisk and confident, excellent at managing staff and working for one of the most efficient companies in his field. His career record was excellent, but his record with girlfriends was not so good. There had been several live-in partners in the past, and Jack was unsure about why these affairs had not lasted.

"I do like Maria a great deal," he told me. "And I know what she's talking about. I'd love to feel really relaxed with someone too, but it's not easy for me. I seriously want to marry and have children, but I don't believe in divorce. My parents got divorced when I was twelve, and my mother was devastated by it.

"For me, living with someone is one thing, but marriage is for life. And since that's the case, it's really got to work out, right from the start."

THERAPIST'S ASSESSMENT

Both Maria and Jack were complaining about a lack of intimacy. Sex for them was pleasant, but each of them felt that it would have to provide them with something more than simple physical satisfaction if their partnership was going to be other than temporary.

Their anxieties were brought to a head by the needs of each of them to make a permanent relationship. But since both were highly assertive and capable, their sense of helplessness was accentuated because this was one of the few situations in their lives where neither of them had a clue how to proceed.

FOSTERING INTIMACY
Intimacy is fostered both by the romance of the surroundings and by the ability of those involved to be open and self-disclosing. Because Maria and Jack were busy, capable individuals, they had learned to compartmentalize their lives. This worked excellently as a method of getting efficiently through their workloads, but it also meant that they were poor at sharing their feelings and their experiences with each other.

Since Maria and Jack were both also highly competitive they had learned, early on, not to reveal anything that might make them vulnerable, for fear that it would be used against them. During my individual discussions with them, I learned that there were, in fact, many things about both of them that, if they were revealed, would make them feel vulnerable.

SELF-DISCLOSURE
In order to open themselves to each other, reaching to their vulnerable inner selves, the couple needed to learn how to self-disclose. I warned them that it was going to feel extremely risky trying to do this, since it meant exposing soft parts of the ego, and that if they were going to succeed, each would have to give a great deal of reassurance to the other.

REASSURANCE
Maria and Jack learned how to give reassurance to each other by using comforting, loving words and touch, and how to get each other to self-disclose and express deeply personal thoughts and emotions. Maria and Jack followed through with these suggestions and ended up with a deeper and more tender relationship, a good basis for marriage.

My program for INCREASING THE PHYSICAL SIDE OF INTIMACY

On the previous pages I've suggested methods of reassuring and opening up to each other in the sharing of feelings. On these pages I suggest you play doctors, using a therapy sequence called the Sexological Exam, which I first learned about in the United States. This helps couples bring their genital sensuality into focus and, in the course of doing so, produces a sometimes extraordinary experience of discovery that draws them closer together. If you need an excuse, to help you to get started, pretend it's a game — you are the doctor and your partner lies on a bed in a warm room while you examine him or her.

Stage   BREASTS AND NIPPLES

In the Sexological Exam, either partner can examine the other. Begin by finding out how the breasts and nipples respond to touching and stroking. Gently stroke each breast, then stroke or lightly press around the area of each nipple, using your fingertips. If the nipples become firm and erect, that shows that they are sensitive to stimulation. And if small pale spots appear on the erect nipples, this indicates high arousal. Any firming and swelling of her breasts denotes arousal.

Stage   PUBIC HAIR PATTERN

After examining your partner's breasts and nipples, transfer your attention to the pubic hair. Examine the pubic hair's abundance and texture, and the area that it covers. Pubic hair patterns and thicknesses can vary greatly from one person to another, taking a variety of shapes ranging from a sparse amount of hair to a luxuriant growth stretching from the abdomen down to the genitals and onto the upper leg.

Pubic hair growth is commonly associated with the amount of free-ranging testosterone (a sex hormone) circulating in the body, and large amounts of testosterone may result in an abundance of body and pubic hair and, in men, can cause baldness on the head.

Stage   THE GENITALS

Hold your partner's penis in one hand and ask him to point out the areas that are most sensitive. Note where these are and ask what stimulation works best for him in these areas. To find the sensitive areas in your partner's vagina, slip your finger in and press gently around the vaginal wall.

PENIS SHAPE   Note the shape of his penis. Contrary to what many people believe, the appearance of a man's penis is as individual as the appearance of his face: penises don't all look the same. Ask him on which side he prefers to wear his penis when dressed, and ask if one side feels more sensitive than the other.

THE URETHRA   Look at the head of the penis. The urethra, the tiny slit from which your partner urinates and ejaculates, should be a healthy red color. On the underside of the penis, at the head, is a central ridge of skin called the frenulum. Ask your partner what kind of sensation he experiences here.

THE VAGINA First place your fingers deliberately but gently on the outside of her labia, then at the opening of her vagina and just inside the vagina, and then on the base, the middle, and top of the pubococcygeus muscle (which is located on the floor of her vagina when she is lying on her back). At each point, ask her how much she would like it if your penis could hit that particular spot during intercourse.

THE PERINEUM On a man the perineum is the area between the testicles and the anus and on a woman it is the area between the vagina and anus; this area is often rich in nerve endings and so may be very sensitive to being stroked. Ring the base of the penis with your fingers and ask your partner what specific sensation there is here, if any. Trace your fingers lightly down his testicles and underneath them, where you will encounter the perineum. Each partner can gently run his or her fingers along the ridge of the perineum and ask how it feels to be stroked there.

Stage   THE ANUS

Imagine the anus to be a clock and press gently but firmly at the hour positions around it. Ask your partner if any of the areas feel sensitive: if they do, remember them when stimulating your partner during later lovemaking.

Finally, you and your partner should practice the squeeze technique on him (page 31), so that both of you can learn thorough control over his erection and ejaculation.

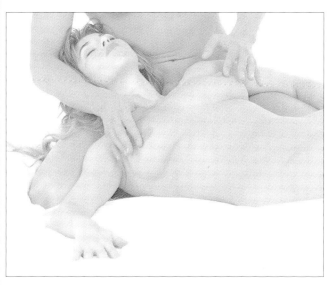

BREASTS AND NIPPLES The exam begins with a check on how your partner's breasts and nipples respond to stimulation. Stroke or lightly press around the area of the nipples to see if they become erect.

ANAL REGION Check the response of your partner's anal region by pressing gently but firmly at the hour positions around the anus. Imagine that the point on the rim of the anus, nearest the vagina or penis, is at the 12 o'clock position. The most sensitive parts of the anus — those that produce the most sensation when they are pressed — will probably be the ten o'clock and two o'clock positions.

GENITAL STROKES Get your partner to show you where the most sensitive parts of his or her genitals are and to demonstrate to you how best to stimulate them, but remember that the object of the exercise is to gain information, not to bring your partner to orgasm.

Use a gentle touch when you are probing your partner's most sensitive parts

PRIVACY AND COMFORT *To do the Sexological Exam in comfort, you need privacy and a warm, draft-free room*

Ask your partner for information and in return tell your partner what your own impressions are

ORAL SEX

There are basically two types of oral sex — licking and sucking of the penis (fellatio) and licking and sucking of the vagina (cunnilingus) — and both are capable of producing ecstatic orgasms. Some members of both sexes find that, for them, oral sex is the most powerful form of sexual stimulation.

FELLATIO Licking the penis as if it were a delicious ice cream cone is the starting point for fellatio. Hold the base of the penis in one hand and then, using the blade of your tongue, lick up from the base of the penis, first on one side and then on the other. After you have repeated this a few times, move on to the famous butterfly flick.

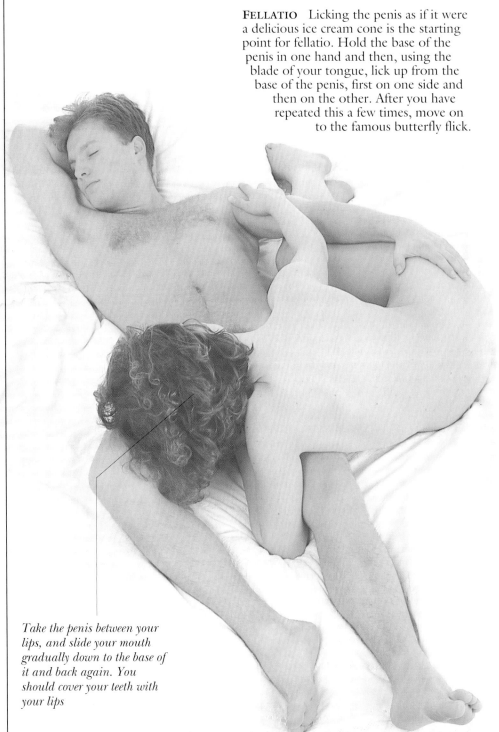

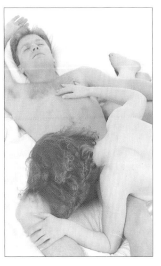

USING YOUR HANDS
When you are reasonably skilled at fellatio you will not need to hold your partner's penis while you do it, which will leave both your hands free to caress him.

Take the penis between your lips, and slide your mouth gradually down to the base of it and back again. You should cover your teeth with your lips

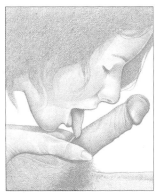

THE BUTTERFLY FLICK
This consists of flicking your tongue lightly across and along the ridge on the underside of the penis.

CUNNILINGUS For really sensational cunnilingus, your head needs to be right between her thighs and preferably slightly below them so that you can stroke your tongue upward against the shaft of her clitoris. From here you can also occasionally insert your tongue into her vagina. Experiment with the tip of the tongue, then the side of the tongue. Try stimulating one side of the clitoris and then the other, always from underneath. Ask her for feedback so that you learn which she likes best.

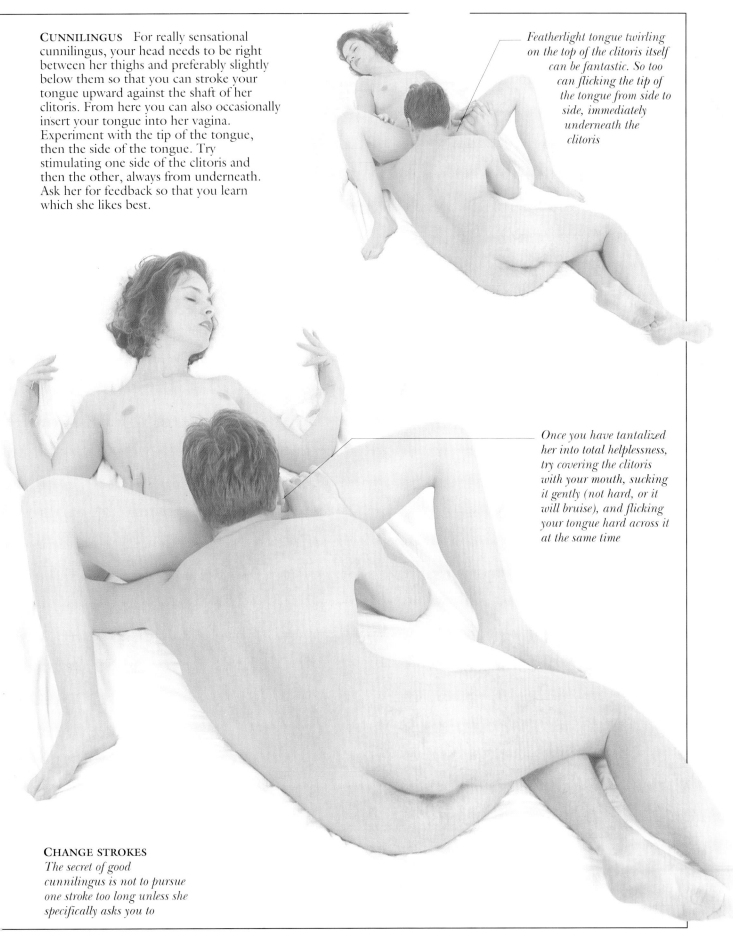

Featherlight tongue twirling on the top of the clitoris itself can be fantastic. So too can flicking the tip of the tongue from side to side, immediately underneath the clitoris

Once you have tantalized her into total helplessness, try covering the clitoris with your mouth, sucking it gently (not hard, or it will bruise), and flicking your tongue hard across it at the same time

CHANGE STROKES
The secret of good cunnilingus is not to pursue one stroke too long unless she specifically asks you to

MUTUAL MASTURBATION DURING LOVEMAKING: 1

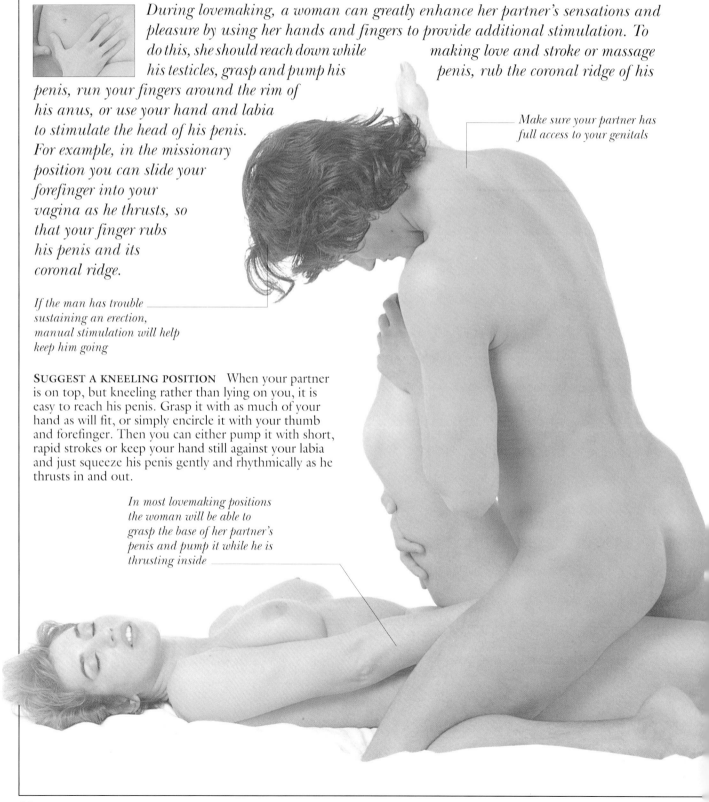

During lovemaking, a woman can greatly enhance her partner's sensations and pleasure by using her hands and fingers to provide additional stimulation. To do this, she should reach down while making love and stroke or massage his testicles, grasp and pump his penis, rub the coronal ridge of his penis, run your fingers around the rim of his anus, or use your hand and labia to stimulate the head of his penis. For example, in the missionary position you can slide your forefinger into your vagina as he thrusts, so that your finger rubs his penis and its coronal ridge.

If the man has trouble sustaining an erection, manual stimulation will help keep him going

Make sure your partner has full access to your genitals

SUGGEST A KNEELING POSITION When your partner is on top, but kneeling rather than lying on you, it is easy to reach his penis. Grasp it with as much of your hand as will fit, or simply encircle it with your thumb and forefinger. Then you can either pump it with short, rapid strokes or keep your hand still against your labia and just squeeze his penis gently and rhythmically as he thrusts in and out.

In most lovemaking positions the woman will be able to grasp the base of her partner's penis and pump it while he is thrusting inside

With eyes closed you can encourage fantasies that enhance your reactions

Having your buttocks fondled and stroked is a highly arousing sensation

STROKE THE ANAL REGION When you are on top of your partner in a position such as this one, you will be able to lean back in order to stroke the rim of his anus with a fingertip and to stimulate his perineum.

KEEP ONE HAND FREE Before making love in a rear-entry position that involves you kneeling or bending over, get your partner to support you securely so that you will have a free hand with which to masturbate him. The easiest way to give your hand access to his genitals is by reaching back between your legs, and you can reach around behind you to caress his buttocks.

GAIN EASY ACCESS When you are astride your partner with your back to him, it is very easy to reach the base of his penis to squeeze it as he thrusts, or to masturbate him during intercourse.

FONDLE HIS TESTICLES Massage his testicles gently from underneath, cupping them loosely in the palm of your hand. This is not hard to do when you are making love while you are on top, astride him and with your back to him, and he opens his legs.

MUTUAL MASTURBATION DURING LOVEMAKING: 2

One great benefit of the so-called sexual revolution of the 60s and 70s was the realization of the value of masturbation for women. Men have always known that it feels good to fondle yourself, and now women are finding that they are more likely to experience orgasm from masturbation than from intercourse. If a woman knows what type of masturbation works best for her, she is in an excellent position to convey this useful information to her lover. Ask your partner what really turns her on and, while you are making love, make sure you give her maximum pleasure by masturbating her in that way.

Insinuate your body against your partner, maintaining contact at all times

ADOPT A SUITABLE POSITION Rear-entry lovemaking positions allow you to reach around easily to your partner's genital area. Because you are entering her from the rear, your partner's clitoris will not be getting any stimulation from direct contact with your pubic area as it would if you were making love face-to-face.

The slow exploration of hands around your genitals during intercourse will be unbelievably arousing

Continue to pat and stroke her buttocks, mimicking the movements of your hand on her genitals

Use a fingertip to massage your partner's clitoris during lovemaking; this is a very effective way of exciting her and bringing her to orgasm

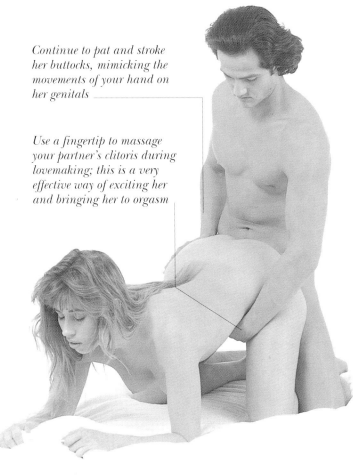

STIMULATE HER CLITORIS Clitoral massage is especially useful when you are making love in this rear-entry position. Every woman has her own preferences when it comes to clitoral massage, so ask your partner if you are doing what she likes best.

DON'T BE AFRAID TO SHOW YOUR INTEREST If you are able to see what you are doing while you are masturbating your partner, and you can watch her reactions, it adds extra excitement to your lovemaking.

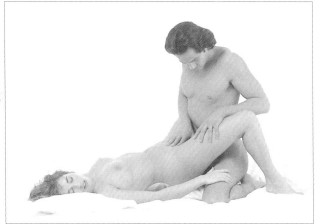

VARY YOUR ACTIONS Extend your caressing and stimulation of your partner beyond her genital area — for example, by gently stroking her belly and running your fingers along the insides of her thighs.

KEEP YOUR HANDS FREE In any lovemaking position where you lie flat on your back with your partner on top of you, you will have both hands free and so will be able to masturbate her, and to stroke and fondle her breasts and nipples.

HOW CAN I REVIVE A PARTNER'S WANING INTEREST?

"A decline in spontaneous desire can be compensated for by imaginative stimulation."

ONE OF THE great destroyers of marriages and other long-term personal relationships is sexual boredom. Age plays a physical part here, and the effects of advancing age on sexual desire and performance are not often anticipated by couples when they are still comparatively young.

Yet people who are in their late thirties and early forties may, without realizing it, be experiencing subtle health and hormonal changes that are progressively reducing their capacity for erogenous sensation. In plain terms, this means that they will need stronger stimulation in order to enjoy sex as much as they formerly did.

The effects of aging cannot, of course, be avoided, but we can come to terms with them and, by adopting suitable attitudes and strategies, prevent them from ever taking the fun and excitement out of our sex lives.

CASE STUDY *Jules & Angie*

Jules was a workaholic, spending many extra hours in the office and frequently working over weekends. This, combined with the effects of age, stress and fatigue, had begun to impede Jules's sex drive and put his marriage to Angie in jeopardy.

Name:	JULES
Age:	40
Marital status:	REMARRIED
Occupation:	ARCHITECT

In spite of his receding hairline and a slight weight problem, Jules was a good-looking man who exuded energy and enthusiasm.

"Angie's my second wife," he told me. "We have two youngsters — they're five and three — and we live in an idyllic spot with every luxury and comfort you can think of. When I come home from work, I want to be able to switch off from all the stresses of the office and enjoy myself with the family. Part of that enjoyment is my sex life with my wife, and yet I don't often feel sexually interested these days.

"I don't understand it. Angie is as gorgeous-looking as she always was, there's no loss of interest on her part, and everything functions wonderfully once I make the effort and get going. But why is it so difficult for me to get started? I'm worried about the long-term effect this will have on Angie. I couldn't face going through another divorce."

Name:	ANGIE
Age:	36
Marital status:	MARRIED
Occupation:	HOUSEWIFE

Angie was a classic blond beauty with wide blue eyes, a model's body with long, shapely legs, and a loving and amenable nature. She adored her husband and children and appeared unspoiled by wealth.

"I've been racking my brains to understand what's going wrong between us," she said. "And I wonder if it's a stress problem. Jules is very stressed by work, and in spite of what he says about leaving it behind at the end of the day, he finds it very hard to unwind. I get a lot of stress too. In spite of having wonderful help, the kids are exhausting at this age, especially since the youngest doesn't sleep, and a lot of the time I'm wandering around like a zombie.

"I know this means I don't have so much energy to put into our lovemaking, but there's not a lot I can do about that. I do make a special point of getting a couple of nights' sleep toward the end of the week, when the nanny takes over, so that I'm fresh for the weekend. But by then Jules doesn't want anything to do with me."

THERAPIST'S ASSESSMENT

Angie's description of Jules as being much more stressed than he admitted was an important insight. Stress can actually alter the body's testosterone levels, which are linked to sexual interest and response, so Jules might have been laboring under a physical disadvantage.

PHYSICAL AND SITUATIONAL PRESSURES

But even without the effects of increasing stress levels, older men often need greater physical stimulation. Without that, it naturally would become more difficult for him to enjoy good erotic sensation, and as a result he would have less and less incentive to start proceedings in the first place. Angie's good looks and attractive figure had been enough stimulation for him six years earlier, but now he needed something more.

Angie, on the other hand, was struggling with the fatigue that all mothers of young children will recognize. When you are constantly exhausted, it is very hard to turn into a temptress at the end of the day. Angie, however, is in a more fortunate situation than most, since she can afford a nanny. Her scheme of having the nanny look after the kids two nights of the week, giving her a chance to catch up on her sleep, was a wise one; it gave her the energy she needed to revive her own interest in sex. But, as she had discovered, there is never any guarantee that one partner's renewed interest in lovemaking will rekindle the other's.

STIMULATING MIND AND BODY

Jules's options were to try and rethink what was happening to him in regard to work, to seek extra rest himself, and to work out with Angie what some of his most sensuous and erotic desires might be, so that they could bring these into their lovemaking.

As part of the enhancement program, Angie focused particularly on giving Jules strong penile stimulation by hand, not something she'd ever done previously. Yet it turned out to be one of the most exciting and erotic experiences he had ever enjoyed. Having this to look forward to did not mean he felt desire in the spontaneous manner of earlier years, but it did mean he was delighted to set aside regular time each week for a wonderful sensuality session.

My program for
USING SUGGESTION AS A TURN-ON

One of the greatest arts of lovemaking lies in using the power of suggestion to such effect that a partner is turned on to the point of orgasm before you've even laid a finger on him or her. If, as you proceed to pay attention to their body, you talk them through a scenario, letting your fingers (or any other part of your body) enact your words, you can create a sense of anticipation so overwhelming your partner will go wild with excitement.

Stage 1 — ESTABLISH YOUR GUIDELINES

The secret of success is to be absolutely in charge of the story and not to let up despite the reaction of your lover. Having said that, it is vital that before you let loose with your imagination you have a very clear idea of what is going to be acceptable to your lover and what isn't. If you don't know what activities are likely to be acceptable, you need to find out well in advance.

GUIDELINES One couple, developing their interest in mild bondage and spanking, drew up some clear guidelines. If either of them shouted, "Stop!" or "No!" or "I can't bear it any longer!" or any permutation of these, they agreed to take no notice.

If, on the other hand, the partner being dominated spoke an agreed code word when he or she wanted to stop, that was serious stuff — it meant that all activities should cease immediately. They stuck to the agreement, and it worked.

TRUST It worked, of course, because the two trusted each other completely. If you are going to put yourself into someone's power and allow them total control of your body, even if it is only for a short time, you need to have developed an exceptionally trusting relationship with that person.

One sex researcher even described such a pairing as the height of emotional trust — a very different view from the seamy image that mild spanking relationships have had in the public mind.

Stage 2 — PLAN A SUGGESTIVE SCENARIO

Some people like to plan their scenario in advance. One person actually made reminder lists which included such items as "Leave sharp objects like scissors and knives in conspicuous places." The mere reading of this reminder makes the premise of such an arrangement clear. What came into your mind when you read that? Suspicion? Apprehension? Anxiety? Whatever it was, you felt something. Your emotions were aroused, which is the whole point. Such is the power of suggestion.

So, by subtly dressing up the meeting place, you can alter it to send some very distinct messages to the person visiting. It is up to you to choose what those might be.

AROUSAL Another arousing move, once you are in bed together, is to tell your partner what is going to happen and then leave things for a while so that expectations are aroused by the wait. The same person who made the reminder list once left a partner waiting for half an hour while he went into a separate room. By the time he returned she was so angry she was fully aroused, sexually as well as emotionally.

GIVING ORDERS One situation that turns some people on is to order them around before every erotic move. For example, in *The Story of O*, O was ordered to stand with her legs slightly apart in front of her master. Just the act of being ordered renders some people a little helpless, a little vulnerable, a little out of control and therefore very erotically aroused.

TAKE IT SLOWLY If you are a complete newcomer to suggestion and role-playing, it's a good idea to progress slowly with your ideas and activities. If at some stage you come to a boundary for either of you, it is vital that this boundary is respected. That doesn't mean to say it shouldn't be examined, even tested, provided the other agrees, but when finally one of you says, "This is my limit," that limit must be observed: if it isn't, trust disappears and the relationship is destroyed.

Stage SEXUAL GAMES

The variety of sexual games that you and your partner might want to play is limited only by your combined imaginations and inclinations.

Love games pp 36, 38, 54,

If these are strong enough and you choose suitable imaginary scenarios, you can play an endless variety of sexual games without the need for dressing up or for equipment such as ropes or blindfolds. But the use of such props can make the games more realistic and easier to play, and they may also help you to dream up new scenarios.

And don't feel restricted to a particular scenario once you have begun to enact it. If it evolves into something different, let yourselves be carried along by it — you can never tell what exciting paths it may lead you down.

Using a blindfold enables you to play tricks on your partner as part of your sexual games

SEXY GAMES TO PLAY

Here are some suggestions for sexy games you might like to play, or you can use them as a basis for your own imaginative inventions.

• Agree that you will do whatever activity your partner orders.

• Take turns (for example, on alternate nights) doing anything enjoyable and sexual with each other *except* for intercourse.

• Try a bit of role-playing: pretend that she's a shy, totally inexperienced young virgin, and he's a sophisticated seducer.

• Pretend that he's an inexperienced youth and she is a seductive older woman.

• Give your partner boundaries for behavior and punish them if they move beyond them. One punishment might be light spanking. (The game is more fun if the boundaries that you choose are impossible to stick to.)

• Tie your partner to the bed with silken cords and tickle and tease to climax.

• Blindfold your partner and announce that he or she must obey you precisely. Tell them that they are going to be the sexual slave of you and another person and that your partner will not know which of you will be having their way with them. There will, in fact, be no other person present, but the key to making this game a success is to convince your partner that there is. In order to do this you will either need to disguise your voice or, better still, not use it. Tread differently, behave differently sexually in your other persona. Penetrative sexual toys such as vibrators, dildos, and anal vibrators, anything safe, can come into their own in this game, provided that you use them gently and carefully and that you are sure your partner has no objections to their use.

• Another version of the blindfold game is to tie your partner face down across a bed or even across a comfortable stool. You tell your partner that you have decided to invite some friends over for the evening (friends your partner has never met) and that you will be with them in the next room. One or more of them may be using your partner's body, you say, during the evening. When you subsequently enter the room disguised, if you want to be really convincing in your role as a stranger you can put a scarf across your mouth. When talking through it you will sound different.

INVENTIVE LOVE GAMES

The use of unusual sexual techniques is often necessary when sexual tension is low and partners feel the need to reinvigorate their desire for each other. Symbolic aggression, in the form of gentle bondage, for instance, often finds favor with both men and women, once they overcome the understandable fear of showing that they like to dominate another person or that they enjoy being dominated. Like most other natural drives, sexual excitement is increased by restraint — but this should never get out of hand. If there is any sign that your partner is not enjoying what you are doing, stop at once.

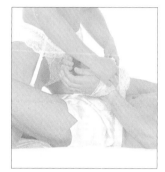

TIE HANDS GENTLY Use scarves, ribbons, pajama cords, or stockings to bind your partner's hands. Other areas where compression boosts sexual feeling are the ankles, elbows, soles of feet, thumbs, and big toes.

TANTALIZE YOUR PARTNER Once he or she is immobilized, teasingly caress the length of his or her body as you will. Your partner shouldn't know what to expect or when, which will increase suspense and sensations immeasurably.

HINTING AT RESTRAINT A scarf or tie used to pull your partner gently closer is a loving way of showing him or her that you need some attention.

Encourage your partner's responses by telling him how much you are being turned on

Slide under your partner's arms and rub your body against his

EMPHASIZE YOUR DOMINANCE Manipulate your partner into positions that serve to show how powerless he or she is to resist your attentions.

If you are uncertain about whether you enjoy being restrained, your legs can be left untied for a quick getaway

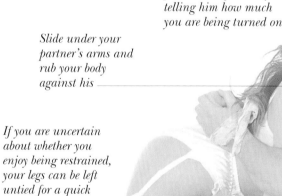

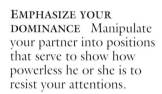

BE GENTLE AND LOVING
Always treat your partner tenderly. The object is to excite, never to hurt or frighten.

Pretend to struggle against your bonds; this can be very exciting for your partner

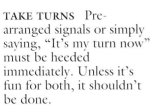

TAKE TURNS Pre-arranged signals or simply saying, "It's my turn now" must be heeded immediately. Unless it's fun for both, it shouldn't be done.

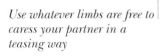

Use whatever limbs are free to caress your partner in a teasing way

DON'T BE TOO SERIOUS A little light relief lets your partner know that this is fun and you are enjoying his or her attentions. You can only play games of this type if you are very secure with your partner.

REVIEW THE EXPERIENCE If you've managed to inject further passion into your lovemaking, and both of you have found the technique useful, you should agree how you'll continue in the future. If, however, one of you has found it distasteful, it should be dropped from your repertoire.

Express your feelings so that you both feel comfortable with the experience

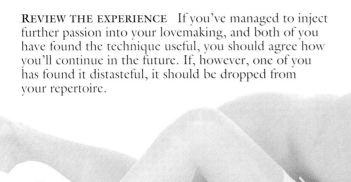

GIVING HIM A SENSUAL MASSAGE

Massage can lay the foundations for relaxation, but once the quality of the touch itself is changed — from using a firm hand to fingertip skimming, from working on the whole body to touching tantalizingly around the genitals — the experience shifts from relaxation to arousal. (For the basic massage strokes, see pages 32-35.)

LEGS AND BACK Begin the session with your partner lying face down, and sit astride his legs. Use warm massage oil to make your hands and his skin slippery and sensuous, and start by leaning back and drawing your hands along the soles of his feet and over his ankles and calves. Then work up from his thighs to his neck.

Use all the basic massage strokes, first firmly, then with relaxed pressure, and finally with light fingertip pressure

LOWER BACK Using gentle, erotic pressure, work your hands slowly up from his thighs and buttocks to his lower back.

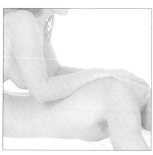

UPPER BACK Pay special attention to the muscles between his shoulder blades and at the base of his neck.

If your bed is too soft, put a comforter or folded blankets on the floor and give your massage there

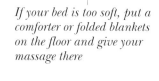

BODY CONTACT When you have finished massaging his back and shoulders, lean forward on to him and slowly and sensuously slide your body from side to side against his. Tighten your thighs against his, and rub your breasts softly across his back.

FRONTAL MASSAGE Ask your partner to roll over onto his back and then, again using plenty of warm oil, massage his abdomen and chest. Lightly massage his breasts and nipples, but avoid touching his genital area.

HEIGHTEN HIS AROUSAL Turn your partner on by first running your fingers lightly around his breasts. Then circle his nipples with featherlight strokes of your fingers, and gently caress their tips. If your hair is long enough, let it trail seductively across his naked body.

Intensify his pleasure by gently gliding your hands up the sides of his chest and along his soft underarm skin

Stroke his face and neck, using your fingertips to trace the outline of his lips, eyes, cheeks, and ears

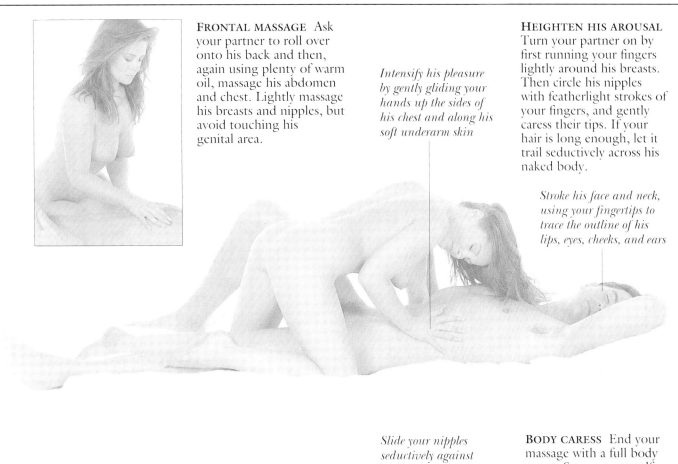

BODY CARESS End your massage with a full body caress. Support yourself on your hands and knees, and lower your body until it is just touching your partner's. Then move slowly from side to side, caressing him with your breasts and belly. Finish off by sliding your body up and down his, then finally sweeping your hands up over his belly

Slide your nipples seductively against his naked skin

Any "accidental" brushing of your body against his genitals will be a highly tantalizing sensation for him

Use your thigh muscles to help you keep your full weight off your partner as you slide against him

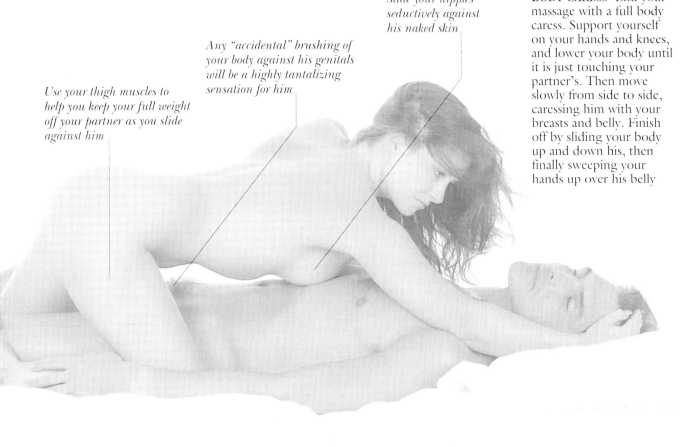

GIVING HER A SENSUAL MASSAGE

Giving your partner a loving, sensual massage will reinforce the bonds of love between you, and it will be a highly erotic experience for both of you. Make yourselves comfortable in a warm, draft-free room, and if your bed is too soft put a comforter or folded blankets on the floor and give her your massage there. (For details of the basic massage strokes, see pages 32-35.)

START AT THE BUTTOCKS
The female buttocks are rich in nerve endings, so they are highly erogenous. Using warm massage oil to make your hands and her skin slippery and sensuous, lightly run the flats of your hands across each of her buttocks.

BACK MASSAGE Put your hands on each side of her hips, thumbs pointing toward her spine, and gently glide them up the sides of her body toward her shoulders. Do this several times, then repeat with your hands flat on her back.

Use all the basic massage strokes, first firmly, then increasingly lightly until your fingertips are just brushing her skin

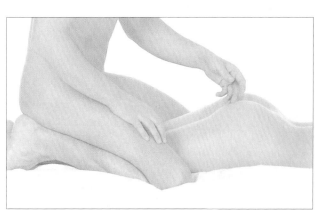

INNER THIGHS Using well-oiled fingers, stroke firmly up the inside of each thigh in turn, from just above the knee up to the buttocks and back. Use only the lightest of finger pressure on the return strokes.

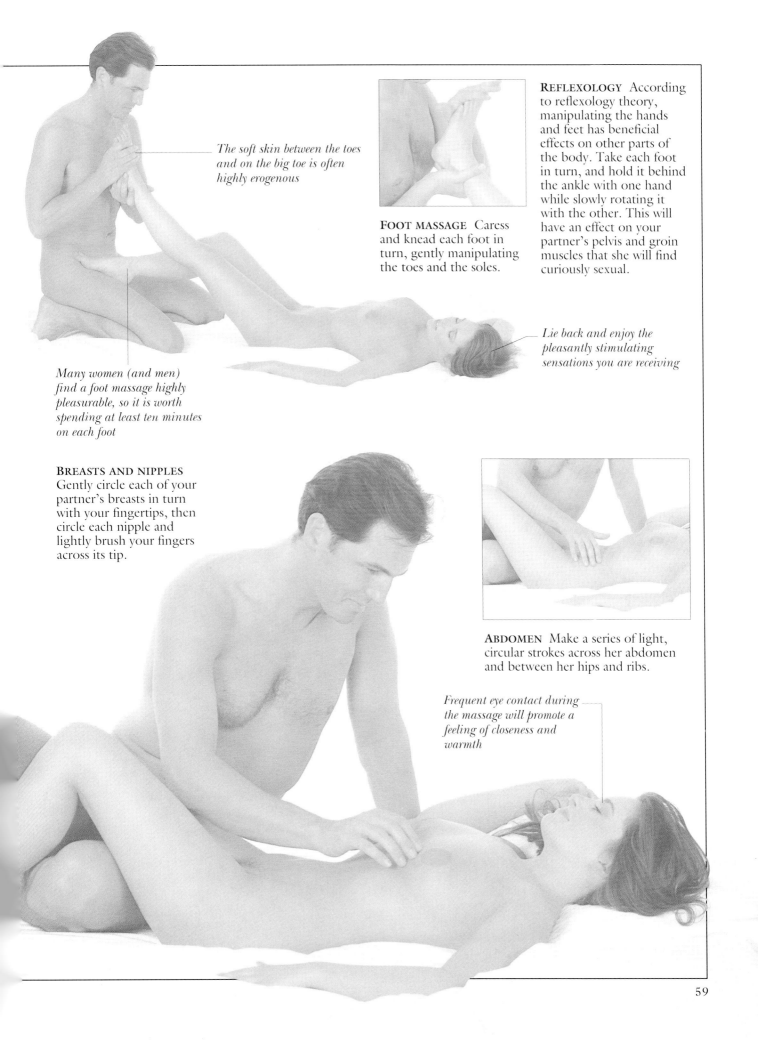

The soft skin between the toes and on the big toe is often highly erogenous

FOOT MASSAGE Caress and knead each foot in turn, gently manipulating the toes and the soles.

REFLEXOLOGY According to reflexology theory, manipulating the hands and feet has beneficial effects on other parts of the body. Take each foot in turn, and hold it behind the ankle with one hand while slowly rotating it with the other. This will have an effect on your partner's pelvis and groin muscles that she will find curiously sexual.

Lie back and enjoy the pleasantly stimulating sensations you are receiving

Many women (and men) find a foot massage highly pleasurable, so it is worth spending at least ten minutes on each foot

BREASTS AND NIPPLES Gently circle each of your partner's breasts in turn with your fingertips, then circle each nipple and lightly brush your fingers across its tip.

ABDOMEN Make a series of light, circular strokes across her abdomen and between her hips and ribs.

Frequent eye contact during the massage will promote a feeling of closeness and warmth

HOW CAN I KEEP SEX SAFE WITH A NEW PARTNER?

"AIDS has forced us to change our sexual habits. Promiscuity threatens not only ourselves but, through us, it threatens others."

BECAUSE OF the spread of sexually transmitted diseases, especially of herpes and AIDS, you cannot afford to take risks with unprotected intercourse. If you want to avoid the risk of infection with HIV (the virus that causes AIDS), you might find that you have to make distinct changes in your dating habits. Instead of assuming that intercourse is going to be available immediately, assume that it isn't. Focus on what used to be called, in the old days, "heavy petting." It may not be the same as intercourse, but mutual masturbation, and using fingers instead of the penis, can lead to some remarkably satisfactory experiences.

If you or your partner are or have been intravenous drug users, and you shared needles with other users, you cannot be sure that unprotected sex will ever be safe.

It is, of course, possible to have tests, including AIDS tests, which give you a pretty good idea of your sexual health, but even these might not indicate the presence of HIV during the early stages of the infection.

To reduce the risk of infection, using a condom or making love by using methods other than intercourse may prove necessary and sensible. How to handle that and how to make it desirable is, of course, another matter altogether.

CASE STUDY *Andrew*

Andrew had a lot of sexual experience and usually preferred to make love to several different women rather than stick with a single partner. But one of his former lovers had tested HIV positive, and although tests showed that he was free of the infection, the episode had made him scared to have sex.

Name:	ANDREW
Age:	36
Marital status:	SINGLE
Occupation:	ENGINEER

"There's nothing like thinking you may actually have caught HIV to change your outlook on life," said Andrew. "Up until then, I had been blatantly promiscuous and I just didn't give a damn about any consequences of my sexual behavior. To be truthful, I didn't think HIV could happen to me — until I was contacted by a hospital tracing department. A voice on the telephone informed me that a girl I'd had a brief affair with some months previously was HIV positive. I was advised to go for testing, and I did so immediately. The days between the call and getting the result of the test were the worst in my life. I was sure that I'd caught it. I've had my share of sexual infections, and I was convinced I'd be HIV positive. I wasn't. I waited three months and then had a second test to make absolutely sure. Thank God, I was all right.

"But I haven't dared to make love to anyone since then. I'm scared. There is no way I'll let myself in for that again, and I might not be so lucky next time. But now I don't know where to start. Do I avoid sex altogether? I certainly don't want to, but if I've got to use condoms I'm going to feel terrible. For one thing, I've always hated the feel of the things. And for another thing, I can't stand their smell.

"I can certainly understand why people prefer a permanent partner nowadays. But my problem is, the better I get to know and like a girl, the less I fancy her. I wish this wasn't the case but it is. What am I going to do?

"My mother would love to see me married, and to tell the truth, sometimes I think that I would like that too. And I'd like to become a dad. So I've got other reasons for wanting to settle down, and sharing a house seems a small price to pay for staying alive and well.

"But I've lived on my own for years now and I suppose I've got accustomed to it. I value my privacy, but I also value my health. I know it won't be easy, but how can I ensure that sex stays safe?"

THERAPIST'S ASSESSMENT

I advised Andrew to become self-revealing, to get comfortable with condom usage, and to make love without intercourse more than formerly. Since these suggestions, by their nature, meant that he was likely to become more intimate with a partner than in the past, he was also likely to form a longer-term relationship.

INTIMACY AND SAFE SEX
If the heat of your passion overcomes you and you want to have intercourse, this is the signal to talk about sexual health. Waving your HIV test certificate would be a way of doing it but not exactly a sensitive one, especially if your partner felt insulted at being asked about his or her sexual health. Leading the conversation around to such questions would be better, and the best way to do this is to begin by talking about your own sexual history rather than asking for details of your partner's. Self-revelation is always the best way to introduce a tricky discussion. I told Andrew that if he could tell his next new partner about his recent unpleasant experience, and use it as an explanation and apology for asking about her, she would most likely understand and sympathize.

SAFER OPTIONS
Lovemaking without intercourse, or intercourse with a condom, really have to be your options. For inspiration on lovemaking without intercourse see page 27, and for details on how to use a condom see page 66. Many people have developed an aversion to the smell of condoms, but it is important to understand that this is a learned response and can be unlearned. You might even find, as some people do, that the rubbery smell of condoms actually becomes erotic because it is associated with a time of great pleasure.

Sometimes the emotional discomfort of getting out the condom and putting it on is the difficulty. This in itself may mirror the lack of trust or of knowledge between the people involved, particularly at the beginning of a relationship. Putting in some time on talking through your views and feelings would go a long way toward making the condom moment easier and acceptable.

Some, usually slightly older, men find that wearing a condom numbs them so that it is hard for them to feel really stimulated, sometimes to such an extent that it is very difficult for them to climax. There are no real answers to this one, except to experiment with different types of condoms in a search for the one that allows most sensitivity.

My program for SAFE SEX

"Safe sex" is the term commonly used to describe forms of sexual activity that are unlikely to expose the participants to HIV infection and thus to AIDS. Safe sex is generally regarded as any form of sexual activity where there is no exchange of bodily fluids between the partners involved — an exchange of bodily fluids being the most common way in which HIV infection is passed from one person to another. But in addition to offering you a high level of protection against HIV infection, safe sex techniques can help to prevent you from catching (or passing on) most other sexually transmitted diseases, including gonorrhea, syphilis, chlamydia, and genital herpes.

Stage — UNDERSTANDING HIV AND AIDS

Once it gets into the bloodstream, HIV — the human immunodeficiency virus — destroys the body's ability to fight disease. The virus invades, and then multiplies in, the white blood cells that play a vital part in the body's immune system, its defense against infection and disease.

AIDS Eventually, the damage to the body's white blood cells reaches a level at which the immune system can no longer function properly. This condition is called AIDS (acquired immune deficiency syndrome) and it makes the body vulnerable to opportunistic diseases, including certain pneumonias and cancers, that are often fatal. The time be-tween initial infection with HIV and the development of AIDS can be up to eight years, and so people who have been infected without knowing it can, through unprotected sex, unwittingly pass it on to other people.

THE SPREAD OF INFECTION The first thing to bear in mind about HIV infection and AIDS is that the problem is not confined to the homosexual community. It is true that in Europe, North America and Australia the gay population has been hardest hit by the infection. But there, as elsewhere in the world, it is becoming increasingly prevalent among heterosexuals. We are all potentially at risk.

HIV TRANSMISSION The most common means by which the human immunodeficiency virus spreads from one person to another is through sexual contact involving

Caress your partner's genitals; it's both safe and pleasurable

SAFE SEX IS ALSO EXCITING Mutual masturbation, coupled with the sharing of your sexual fantasies, is only one of the many "permitted" activities.

the exchange of bodily fluids — that is, the passing of semen, vaginal secretions, or blood from one person to his or her sexual partner. An infected (HIV-positive) man can transmit the virus to his sexual partners — of either sex — because his semen will contain the virus in very large numbers. And a woman who has become infected with HIV can pass the virus on to her subsequent sexual partners because it will be present in her vaginal secretions.

In addition, because the virus is found in the blood of infected people as well as in their semen or vaginal fluid, infected drug addicts can spread the virus relatively easily by sharing hypodermic needles with uninfected friends. There have also been many reported instances of hemophiliacs being infected by transfusions of contaminated blood or blood products, and an HIV-positive mother can pass the infection on to her unborn baby.

ONE MAY BE ENOUGH   The ease with which the infection can pass from one person to another, during unprotected intercourse, is clearly illustrated by the numerous cases in which only a single sexual contact with an infected person, without using any form of protection, has been enough for someone to become infected with HIV.

For example, there has been many a well-documented case in which a woman has contracted HIV through a single sexual contact with a man who, unknown to her, was an intravenous drug addict who had become infected with the virus by sharing his needles with other users.

In a number of other cases, married women have been infected with HIV by their husbands, who caught the virus through having heterosexual or homosexual affairs or as a result of a single unprotected sexual contact with an infected prostitute.

SOURCES OF HIV INFECTION

HIGHEST RISK :

• Vaginal sexual intercourse without a condom

• Anal intercourse with or without a suitable condom

• Fellatio, especially to climax

• Any sexual activity that draws blood, whether accidentally or deliberately

• Sharing penetrative sex aids, such as vibrators

• Inserting fingers or hands into the anus

ACTIVITIES INVOLVING SOME DEGREE OF RISK:

• Vaginal sexual intercourse with a condom

• Love bites or scratching that breaks the skin

• Anal licking or kissing

• Sexual activities involving urination

• Mouth-to-mouth kissing if either partner has bleeding gums or cold sores

• Cunnilingus using a latex barrier

• Fellatio using a condom

RISK-FREE :

• Dry kissing

• Wet kissing as long as neither partner has bleeding gums or cold sores

• Stimulating a partner's genitals with your hands, or having your genitals stimulated by a partner's hands

• Self-masturbation

• Being bitten by a bloodsucking insect

• Sitting on a toilet seat

• Swimming in a pool

• Using other people's bed linen or towels

• Swallowing another person's saliva (assuming there are no cuts or sores in your mouth)

• Sneezing or being sneezed on

• Cheek-to-cheek kissing

• Shaking hands, embracing, or cuddling

• Sharing a glass or cutlery

• Being a blood donor (in developed countries where the needles used are sterilized)

Sensual condom p66

CONDOMS By creating a physical barrier that prevents the exchange of bodily fluids during intercourse, condoms provide a simple way of having "safe sex." Spermicidal jellies and creams help too, because they appear to make the virus less active. So simply by ensuring that we use condoms and spermicides we can greatly reduce the danger of infection with HIV, and also the risk of catching other sexually transmitted diseases.

Stage ASKING FOR SAFE SEX

Put bluntly, the safest ways to avoid AIDS are by choosing to be celibate (unlikely for readers of this book), by careful use of condoms and spermicides, and by engaging in and enjoying the many types of sexual activity that are alternatives to intercourse.

When you are with a partner you know well, suggesting that you use condoms or indulge in non-coital sexual activities is usually not too difficult, but raising the subject with someone new can often be embarrassing and awkward.

ATTITUDES This potential awkwardness is often made worse by the different attitudes people have toward HIV, AIDS, and safe sex. For example, many people erroneously believe that AIDS is not a heterosexual problem and refuse to take precautions. There are many others who understand there are dangers from HIV but feel they are slight, and anyway find it impossible to ask a partner to use a condom or to consider whether or not he or she might have encountered the virus.

On the other hand, some people are fearful of getting HIV and use precautions conscientiously. However, a few take this too far and become phobic about HIV and AIDS and, even in circumstances where they know they cannot possibly have caught the virus, cannot relax until they have had a blood test that shows them to be HIV negative.

HOW TO ASK Some people find it very hard to talk about any aspect of sexuality, let alone to ask whether or not a potential sex partner is HIV free. Indeed, even the most suave among us find this difficult. Unfortunately, for anyone entering a new relationship the tricky and embarrassing HIV/AIDS discussion has to be tackled. Assertiveness helps us deal with tricky situations and establishes feelings of self-worth and value; becoming sexually assertive helps you cope with difficult or uncomfortable situations such as asking a new partner to wear a condom.

When developing a relationship with someone new, try getting comfortable first with small aspects of sexuality. Tackle them slowly, with the easiest discussion first. Remember that self-disclosure (see page 41) is a good way of approaching something difficult.

CONTACT WITH FLUIDS
During masturbation, avoid contact with your partner's semen or vaginal fluids if you have any cuts or open sores on your fingers or hands

PRACTICE NON-PENETRATIVE SEX
Caressing and masturbating a partner are enjoyable alternatives to sexual intercourse.

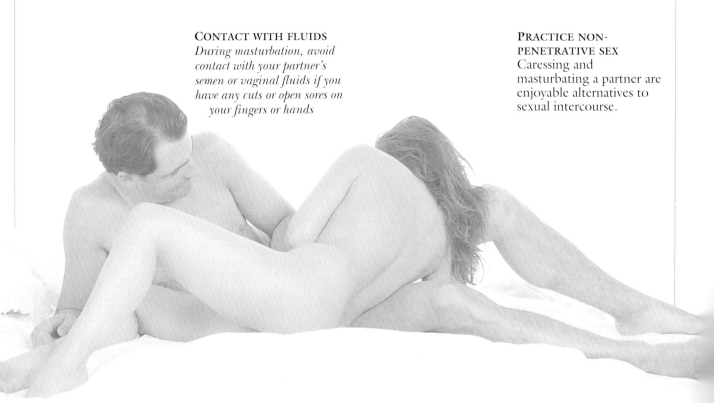

Try phrases such as: "I feel very nervous about asking this question, but it's something that's very important to me." "What's your feeling about safe sex?" "I know some people think women [or young people] shouldn't carry condoms, but I think it's very important. I carry them. Do you?" "I've often wondered about the value of taking an AIDS test. But I've never done it so far. Have you?" "I know some people think I'm too careful, but I really only feel safe with sex when using condoms. How about you?"

SAYING NO It may be that the end result of your delicate and carefully negotiated discussion is that your partner refuses to use condoms or follow other safe sex practices. Here's how you might say no to unprotected sex: "I like you very much and I'd love to go to bed with you, but I feel so strongly about safe sex practices that, under the circumstances, I'm going to have to say no. But why don't we try to stay really good friends?"

ALTERNATIVES TO INTERCOURSE If condoms are not available, or if one or both of you is unwilling to use them, you should avoid having sexual intercourse. But that, of course, doesn't mean you have to abstain from sexual pleasure — there are several very enjoyable sexual activities for you to try that do not involve intercourse.

FANTASY AND MASTURBATION For example, you and your partner could take turns describing your sexual fantasies to each other while you both self-masturbate, or while you masturbate each other. You could both use vibrators, or use vibrators on each other, provided you didn't share them. Or you could simply rub your bodies up against each other, perhaps simulating the movements of intercourse.

ORAL SEX Because there is a fairly high risk of infection, oral sex should be avoided unless you take careful precautions to prevent contact with semen or vaginal fluid. For fellatio, this means using a condom, and for cunnilingus a latex barrier (these are available at some drugstores).

Massaging each other's whole body, including the genitals, is another option, but, as is the case with oral sex, contact with bodily fluids such as semen and vaginal secretions should be avoided, especially if you have any skin cuts into which the fluids could penetrate.

HIV/AIDS QUESTIONS

Q. Isn't it only homosexuals who get AIDS?

A. No, not at all. This notion arose in Western countries because the first cases of AIDS to be diagnosed, in the early 1980s, were among homosexual males in the United States. Since then, the majority of cases in the West have involved gay men, but elsewhere (for instance in Africa) the majority of people affected are heterosexual. And because, in general, the gay community has adopted a responsible attitude toward safe sex, the rate of increase in the number of AIDS cases in the West is now higher among heterosexuals than among homosexuals.

Q. If my partner and I are both virgins and neither of us are hemophiliacs or drug users, we don't need to use condoms, do we?

A. There are other possible, but extremely rare, ways to catch HIV, such as through infected and improperly sterilized dental or surgical equipment, or if blood from an infected person gets into an open cut or scratch on your skin, for example, during a fight or when playing a sport that involves hard physical contact.

But these are, as I mentioned, incredibly rare and there is likely to be hardly any risk for you in intercourse without condoms. That is, as long as you are certain you are both monogamous. The problem arises, of course, when you think a partner is sexually faithful when, in fact, he or she has been deceiving you. There has been more than one tragic case of a woman who has only ever slept with one man in her entire life, i.e., her husband, but who nevertheless discovers one day that she has AIDS.

Q. Can lesbians get HIV?

A. It is possible that women can transmit the virus to other women but it is extremely rare. There have been, so far, only a tiny number of cases reported.

Q. I have heard that HIV is a very fragile organism and is actually hard to get. Is this true?

A. Yes. It cannot live outside the body very long, which is why it can't be transmitted by shaking hands or caught from lavatory seats.

Q. Is it true that women get HIV easier than men?

A. It is not known yet whether this is a hard-and-fast rule but, in general, since there are far more men infected it means that women are now at greater risk. A woman is more likely to meet an infected man than vice versa.

THE SENSUAL CONDOM

The condom is not only an effective form of contraceptive, it also acts as a barrier to infection with sexually transmitted diseases such as syphilis, gonorrhea, chlamydia, and HIV — putting on a condom correctly can thus sometimes mean the difference between safety and sickness. Some couples, however, are reluctant to use condoms because they think that interrupting their lovemaking to put one on is unromantic and unerotic. But by following a few simple rules, a woman can turn the mundane act of slipping a condom onto her partner's penis into a truly erotic experience.

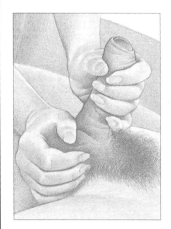

CHOOSING CONDOMS
As a general rule, avoid unknown brands and always check the expiration date on the package. Avoid the strangely shaped condoms with knobbly edges and clitoral ticklers — although they heighten the sensation they are, alas, generally unsafe because they do not fit the penis tightly enough and so may slip off or allow semen to leak into the vagina during intercourse

START WITH A GENITAL MASSAGE   To make the donning of the condom as erotic an experience as possible, begin by treating your lover to a brief but sensuous genital massage.

When slipping a condom onto your lover's penis, use slow, sensuous movements to make the occasion as erotic as possible

MASTURBATE HIM
Change your hand action from genital massage to gentle masturbation of him as a preliminary to slipping the condom onto his penis.

Make putting on a condom part of foreplay; don't wait until your excitement gets the better of you

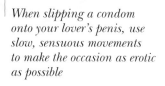

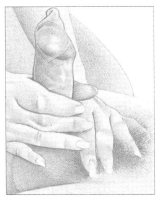

SQUEEZE OUT THE AIR
Gently press the tip of the condom between thumb and forefinger to ensure it contains no air — an air bubble could cause it to split during intercourse.

PUT ON THE CONDOM
Put it on the tip of his penis with one hand and roll it down to the base with the other. If he is uncircumcised, first push back his foreskin.

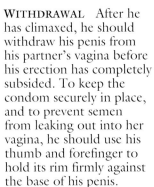

WITHDRAWAL   After he has climaxed, he should withdraw his penis from his partner's vagina before his erection has completely subsided. To keep the condom securely in place, and to prevent semen from leaking out into her vagina, he should use his thumb and forefinger to hold its rim firmly against the base of his penis.

USING CONDOMS   Condoms should be used to make oral sex safe (above) as well as to provide protection during intercourse (below). For oral sex, use flavored condoms to make the act of giving fellatio through a condom more enjoyable for her.

You may find that using a condom helps you to maintain your erection longer and delays ejaculation

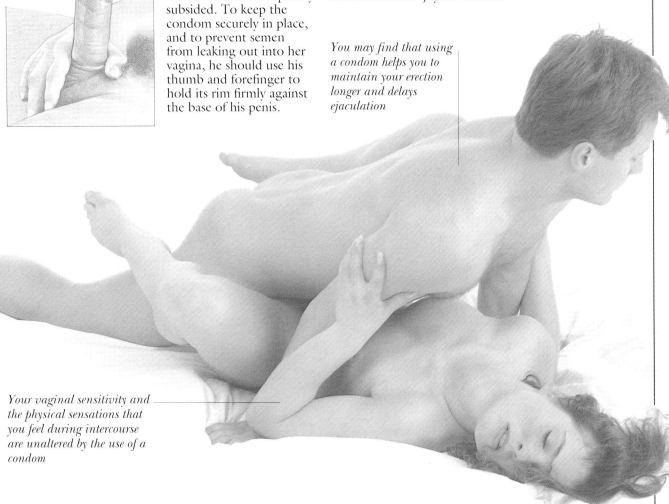

Your vaginal sensitivity and the physical sensations that you feel during intercourse are unaltered by the use of a condom

HOW CAN I ACHIEVE A DEEPER ORGASM?

"A feeling of warmth, security, and closeness is one of the essential elements in setting the scene for sexual bliss."

IT IS POSSIBLE that to experience bliss, whether sexual or any other kind, we shouldn't look for it too often. If it became commonplace it would lose its special value, because it would then be expected and almost predictable, with a consequent lessening of the wonderful excitement that it brings when it takes us unawares.

Outstanding lovemaking undoubtedly depends on a combination of factors, including surprise. One thing that can't be planned is surprise, but many of the other factors that combine to make lovemaking outstanding can be deliberately invoked.

Among these are feelings of relaxation and security, which are, in most cases, easy to generate. Among the main ingredients of sexual relaxation are physical and emotional relaxation; a sense of being entirely in harmony with each other; a feeling of physical warmth and comfort; mutual caressing; and being able to take your time over your lovemaking.

CASE STUDY *Hayley & Richard*

Hayley and Richard had both, individually, sometimes experienced unusually deep and strong feelings during orgasm. This only seemed to happen by accident, and what they both wanted to know was — how could they make such intense and satisfying feelings happen more often?

Name:	HAYLEY
Age:	33
Marital status:	SINGLE
Occupation:	COPYWRITER

Hayley was in her second long-term relationship. She was agile and gypsylike, with short, curly black hair and punkish but extremely expensive clothes.

"Richard and I have been together for three years," she told me. "And we are pretty committed to each other. We have a very similar outlook on life and, although it sounds corny, this is partly a spiritual one. By that I mean we have a similar sense of morality and feel strongly that we want something spiritual out of our life together.

"Which brings me to sex. The best sex for me has been when I have been deeply relaxed and at the same time very focused on the sexual sensation while it is building up. I feel very far away in my head when I finally come to orgasm, and the climax seems to come from somewhere incredibly deep down inside of me.

"This is a wonderful experience, but it doesn't happen very often, and only ever by accident. Is there any way of encouraging it?"

Name:	RICHARD
Age:	30
Marital status:	SINGLE
Occupation:	INSTRUMENT MAKER

Richard was a former naval officer who had set up his own business as a maker of naval brass instruments such as sextants. He was comfortable with new acquaintances and felt at home with both 18-year-olds and 80-year-olds.

"I felt when I met Hayley that she had no pretensions. She was completely open to me, in spite of a sharp difference between her earning power and status and mine. She is very senior in her company and very successful. But there's no sense of competition or one-upmanship from her.

"I know what she means about wanting this deeper feeling during orgasm. It's happened to me too. I personally doubt you can achieve it deliberately. With me, it's always happened as a result of a long, peaceful buildup. Maybe we'll talk in bed, for a long time sometimes, while caressing each other, and one thing leads to another. That's great. But it's accidental."

THERAPIST'S ASSESSMENT

In my discussions with Hayley and Richard, I stressed that there were no specific answers to their question. When lovemaking works unusually well, the unexpectedness of this adds poignancy and deeper feeling to climaxes. We may not be able to plan this surprise, but we do know that we can create some of the other ingredients for deeply relaxed lovemaking.

Feelings can be aroused by a variety of techniques. For example, anticipation, mild anxiety, anger, and passion can all be deliberately induced. So in order to create extreme sexual relaxation, it is worth identifying its ingredients. These will, of course, differ from one couple to another, but those that Hayley and Richard identified, when they sat down and made a list of their emotions and activities, are fairly typical. They listed:
• open-ended time
• warmth
• the comfort of their king-sized bed
• restful lighting
• mutual caresses during conversation
• awareness of each other's mental state (it is hard to be erotic if you are worried or angry about something)
• an ability to pick up on sexual areas where one partner is asking for encouragement.

KEY POINTS
The most important points, though, were the last two. Among the feelings generated by these ingredients were a sense of nakedness (meaning openness or being entirely exposed to each other) and extreme trust in order to be able to feel this; a kind of telepathic sharing of the same feeling (each could look the other in the eye and know that they too were flooded with a sense of beauty); and a sense, as climax approached, of letting themselves flow off the edge of everyday consciousness into a tumult completely beyond control.

TAKING TIME
Hayley and Richard agreed that the key to this experience was time — the ability to give themselves enough time in which to relax and experience all their "requirements." They resolved to put aside certain weekend mornings or afternoons when they would deliberately cut themselves off from interruptions, for instance, by unplugging the phone and disconnecting the doorbell. Then they would just spend time together and see what happened.

My program for
INCREASING SEXUAL
FEELINGS

The depth and breadth of sexual feelings between you and your partner can be magnified by taking turns giving each other sensual pleasure without expecting anything in return. This unselfish giving of sensual pleasure involves the use of touch and massage, a gentle, loving form of sexual intercourse that is intended primarily for the benefit of one partner alone.

Stage 1   GIVING PLEASURE

Such is the great emphasis placed on reaching orgasm these days that it is easy to forget that many wonderful and satisfying experiences can be reached through sexual activity not aimed at resolution. Watching your lover unfurl, relax, and bask in the sensuality of your unselfish, non-demanding touch is ex-ceptionally rewarding: as the giver of pleasure you gain feelings of love, tenderness, caring, nurturing, and eroticism.

UNSELFISH TOUCH In your role as the unselfish giver of pleasure, you begin by kissing and caressing your partner's naked body, using the strokes and movements that he or she most enjoys. Everything you do should be geared solely to the pleasure of your partner, who should do nothing but lie back and drift off into sensual bliss.

MASSAGE You should continue kissing and caressing your partner lovingly for about fif-teen minutes, and then change roles: you become the receiver of pleasure and your partner the giver. After that, you can move on to give your partner a Three-Handed Mas-sage. This begins as a body massage session — either a basic one (see pages 32-35) or a more erotic sensual type — but it then progresses to become a highly sensuous combination of massage and intercourse.

GIVING AND RECEIVING
This program will show you the truth of the old saying that it is better to give than to receive.

Stage   RECEIVING PLEASURE

The receiver of pleasure absorbs the giver's loving, caring feelings through the skill and texture of his or her touch and relaxes totally, knowing no performance is expected of him or her. Such a deliberate pleasure-giving exercise puts ideas into the receiver's head and provides a blueprint for a treat that he or she could, in turn, let fall upon the giver.

ECSTASY   What exactly does the receiving partner gain from this loving but undemanding sex? Principally, he or she will experience feelings of love and serenity accompanied by greatly heightened sensuality. With the deep sense of inner peace that this receiving of pleasure creates, fine nuances of love and sensation are capable of expanding into great waves of emotion.

For example, the pleasant but unspectacular sensation of receiving a simple caress can enlarge to become an engulfing, prickling feeling of sensuality. In this way, sexual love from a partner can be experienced as an ecstatic rapture of the mind rather than as a localized physical reflex of the genitals.

PASSIVITY   In order for you to give this experience, your partner has to be capable of receiving it. Some people find it peculiarly difficult to lie back and wholeheartedly enjoy pleasure that is aimed at them alone. Some men feel so strongly that theirs is a "doing" role they find it impossible to be passive. And some women are so used to being the carers and donors of pleasure that they cannot relax into acceptance.

One way of finding out where you stand on the idea of being passive is to give a massage and then ask yourself, "Is it easier to touch for my pleasure or for the pleasure of another?" On a second occasion, switch roles, then ask yourself, "Is it easier to give or receive?" Honest answers to these questions will tell you whether or not you are good at being passive and receiving pleasure.

SELFISHNESS   If acceptance of pleasure turns out to be a problem, it may be that you need to learn more about the value of selfishness. Contrary to popular belief, selfishness, in the sense of accepting that it is all right to be pleasured, is healthy. Orgasm is, after all, a supremely selfish experience that no one else can have for you but you.

Stage   GIVING AN EROTIC MASSAGE

A sensual, erotic massage is a very good way to give pleasure, and the better you get to know your partner's body (for instance, by doing the Sexological Exam) the more erotic you can make the massage. To give such a massage, begin with the usual basic strokes such as circling, swimming, and kneading with your thumbs and fingertips.

Sex exam p42

PRESSURE VARIATIONS   Carry out each stroke three times. Use firm pressure to begin with, and then repeat each stroke twice, using first relaxed pressure and then the lightest of fingertip pressure. While you are massaging with firm pressure, work your hands and fingers into your partner's muscles to loosen

TAKING TIME OFF FROM EVERYDAY LIFE

Learning to relax into selfishness often means taking time off from everyday life in order to concentrate on yourself alone. This can be practiced by:

• Having a frank discussion with your partner about respecting the hour you are going to take for yourself.

• Discussing the need for privacy with anyone else in the house.

• Putting a lock or bolt on the door of your room.

• Hanging up a "Do Not Disturb" sign.

• Rescheduling your daily activities to free an hour that you can set aside for yourself.

• Making a place in your home that is warm, welcoming, and sensuous.

• Practising self-pleasuring techniques, such as self massage, including setting aside an hour at least once a week when you do whatever you honestly feel like doing.

It can be surprisingly difficult to carve this free time from your normal routine, but before long you will begin to feel that there ought to be more of it. The onset of that feeling will mark the beginning of a healthy acceptance of the fact that you are entitled to enjoyment. Relaxing into selfishness is a path to sensuality focused on you alone.

them up and relieve any tension in them. This will help him or her to relax, both physically and mentally, and thus become more receptive to the increasingly sensuous pleasure of the rest of the massage.

FACE-DOWN MASSAGE Massage the whole body in this fashion, first with your partner lying face down. Start at the neck and shoulders, and then massage each arm in turn, all the way down to the fingertips.

Next, work your way down your partner's back, over the buttocks and down each leg in turn as far as the ankle. Don't massage the feet at this stage, because that is easier to do when your partner is lying face up.

FACE-UP MASSAGE Turn your partner over onto his or her back, and, as before, begin your massage at the neck and shoulders, working first down the arms and then down the chest and abdomen. As you move nearer to the genitals, occasionally and "accidentally" brush them with the back of your hand, or with any other part of your body that is conveniently close. Then, just as your partner is expecting you to massage the genital area itself, veer away; he or she will probably find this provocative behavior outrageously tantalizing.

THIGHS AND FEET Once you reach the legs, work your way down each in turn and pay special attention to the insides of the thighs, which are highly erogenous. When you get to the feet, in addition to giving each one its individual massage, combine foot massage using one hand with inside thigh massage using the other.

Another pleasant way in which to manipulate your partner's feet is to support each one in turn behind the ankle with one hand, while slowly rotating the foot with the other. The effects are felt all the way up the leg to the pelvis and the groin muscles, and the overall sensation that is produced is curiously sexual.

USE YOUR NAILS If you want to take your sensual massage one stage further, try lovingly caressing your partner all over with your fingernails. Before you begin, make sure that your nails are not broken or rough-edged. Use only your nails on your partner's skin, and move them in a variety of ways so as to maximize their sensual effect. Start off by moving them in circles, then change to up-and-down and side-to-side movements, varying the lengths of the strokes you make from very short to relatively long.

EROTIC HELPLESSNESS During all the stages of your sensual massage, do not let your partner move any part of his or her body. If, for instance, an arm needs to be moved so that you can massage it more easily, move it yourself — part of the eroticism of a good massage (for the person being massaged) lies in the feeling of helplessness it can create.

Stage 4 THE THREE-HANDED MASSAGE

A more advanced way to give sensual pleasure is by intercourse for the benefit of your partner alone. One very special version of this has been termed the Three-Handed Massage by US massage master Ray Stubbs. Stubbs, if not exactly inventing the following idea, certainly put a lot of time and effort into sensitively developing it.

His suggestion to seekers of deep orgasmic feeling is that they should combine the relaxed sensuality of massage with the gentle touch of intercourse. One session may focus on one partner, a second session on the other. The massagee should not try to reciprocate simultaneously because his or her efforts will detract from the inner calm he or she might

Three-Handed Massage p74

otherwise achieve. It is this same inner calm that allows for a deep sensual experience. Here is how a man can give his partner a Three-Handed Massage — the version of the massage that a woman can give her partner is basically similar, and, like this one, it also begins with a basic massage and ends with penetration.

SETTING UP THE MASSAGE Set the massage up as you would a basic one. Give your partner fifteen minutes or so of manual body massage before including her genitals. Don't hurry. Take your strokes slowly and don't aim at orgasm — for either of you. After this manual massage, move on to give her the three-handed version, which begins with a straightforward back massage.

BACK MASSAGE With your lover lying on her front, give her a relaxing back massage. Use plenty of warm massage oil to do so. During this attention, after stroking and caressing her, gently bring your legs across her thighs so that you are sitting on her. In order to have exceptionally smooth and slippery mobility during the massage, lavishly oil your own abdomen, genitals, and thighs.

Without interrupting your sensual massage of her body, let your well-oiled lower half glide backward and forward over her thighs and buttocks so that your genitals are in contact with her skin and, in effect, also massaging her. Do this in a flowing and sensitive fashion to make it as sensuous as possible, like some kind of exquisite dance.

PENETRATION As you continue with this, let your penis find its slippery way between her slightly parted legs and make its own contact with her vagina. Allow yourself to penetrate her exceptionally slowly — the slower you are, the more tantalizing your touch will be. Let your hands and penis slowly massage her simultaneously so that all the movements

blend. Then ask your partner to turn over and lie on her back. When you feel that the time is right, lift her knees up toward her chest and, as you do so, gently and gradually slide your penis back into her again.

Rock your pelvis rhythmically but very slowly, so that your penis thrusts are tantalizingly sensuous, and at the same time use your hands to stroke, caress, and massage every accessible inch of her body. Emphasize, if she starts to thrust in response, that she must take no active part, but should relax and let herself flow (mentally) into the bedclothes rather than move. The more she relaxes and leaves everything to you, the more profound will be her sensation. But don't forget that you are not aiming for orgasm.

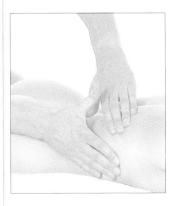

BODY MASSAGE The first step in the Three-Handed Massage is a basic back massage. Spend about fifteen minutes on this, giving your partner slow, sensuous strokes and using plenty of warm massage oil or baby oil. Start with circling, swimming, and glide strokes, and finish off with feathering to enhance the overall effect.

INTERCOURSE When you feel that the time is right for intercourse, gently penetrate her again. As you enter her, lift her knees toward her chest, and rock your pelvis slowly and rhythmically to thrust your penis in and out of her. At the same time, use your hands to stroke and caress and sensuously massage every accessible inch of her naked body.

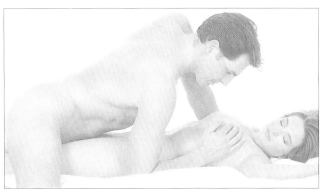

PENETRATION Let your lower body massage her by gliding backward and forward over her thighs and buttocks. Then slip your penis into her vagina, and let it move in and out in time with the massaging movements of your body. Do the same when she turns over.

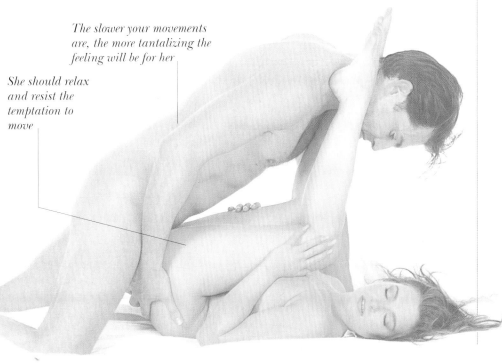

The slower your movements are, the more tantalizing the feeling will be for her

She should relax and resist the temptation to move

THREE-HANDED MASSAGE

The Three-Handed Massage, a concept developed by massage trainer Ray Stubbs, is a combination of sensitive hand massage accompanied by genital contact. For details of the Three-Handed Massage for a female partner see page 72: here the focus is on the sex massage that a woman can give to the man in her life. Because it is his turn to receive, he is in no way to take any active part in what ensues.

SIT ACROSS HIM With your partner lying on his back, straddle him with your thighs across his abdomen. Begin by massaging his chest, arms, and shoulders, and lean back to massage his thighs and as much of his legs as you can reach.

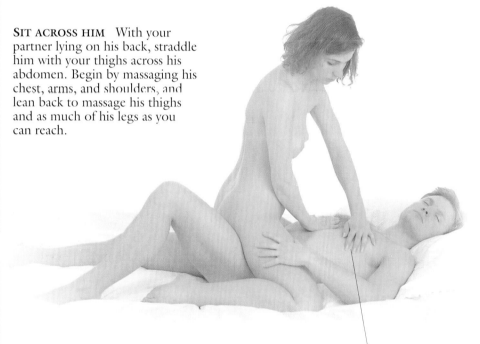

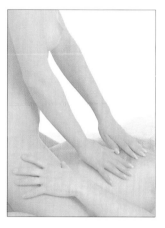

ALTERNATE TOUCHES When you first begin to massage an area, use the palms of your hands. Then, having massaged the whole area with your palms, knead gently with your fingers.

For a slippery sensuousness, oil your hands, genitals, thighs, and abdomen before you begin, and re-oil them as needed during the massage

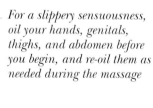

USE SENSUAL BODY MOVEMENTS After massaging him with your hands for about 15 minutes, lightly and provocatively draw your breasts and nipples over his chest, moving them up and down and from side to side.

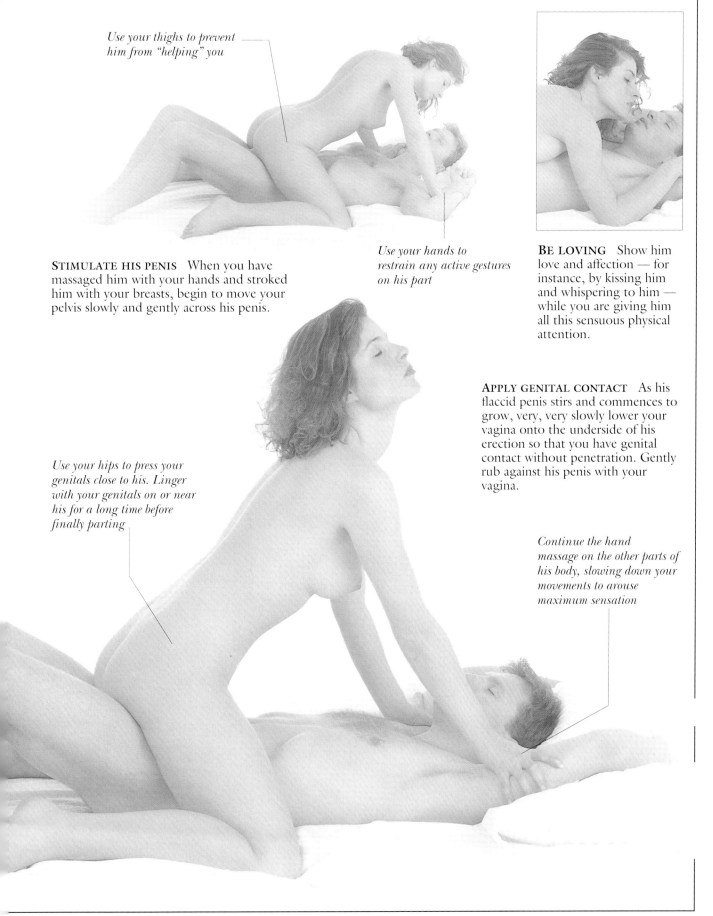

Use your thighs to prevent him from "helping" you

Use your hands to restrain any active gestures on his part

STIMULATE HIS PENIS When you have massaged him with your hands and stroked him with your breasts, begin to move your pelvis slowly and gently across his penis.

BE LOVING Show him love and affection — for instance, by kissing him and whispering to him — while you are giving him all this sensuous physical attention.

APPLY GENITAL CONTACT As his flaccid penis stirs and commences to grow, very, very slowly lower your vagina onto the underside of his erection so that you have genital contact without penetration. Gently rub against his penis with your vagina.

Use your hips to press your genitals close to his. Linger with your genitals on or near his for a long time before finally parting

Continue the hand massage on the other parts of his body, slowing down your movements to arouse maximum sensation

LOVEMAKING ON A CHAIR

Even something as potentially exciting as sex can become boring. By making love on a chair instead of in bed, you can try out a wide range of different lovemaking positions, and perhaps add some welcome variety to your sex life. As a bonus, many of these positions leave your hands free, allowing you to exchange caresses.

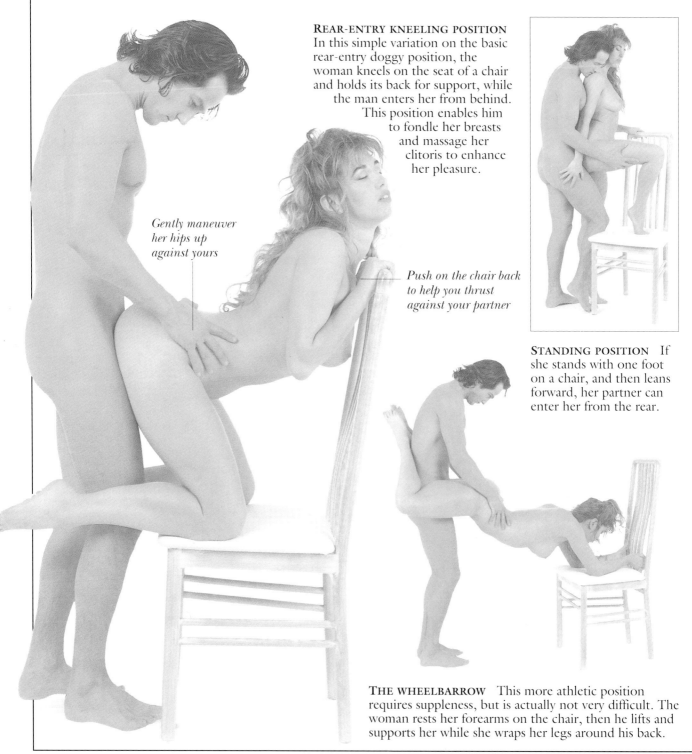

REAR-ENTRY KNEELING POSITION
In this simple variation on the basic rear-entry doggy position, the woman kneels on the seat of a chair and holds its back for support, while the man enters her from behind. This position enables him to fondle her breasts and massage her clitoris to enhance her pleasure.

Gently maneuver her hips up against yours

Push on the chair back to help you thrust against your partner

STANDING POSITION If she stands with one foot on a chair, and then leans forward, her partner can enter her from the rear.

THE WHEELBARROW This more athletic position requires suppleness, but is actually not very difficult. The woman rests her forearms on the chair, then he lifts and supports her while she wraps her legs around his back.

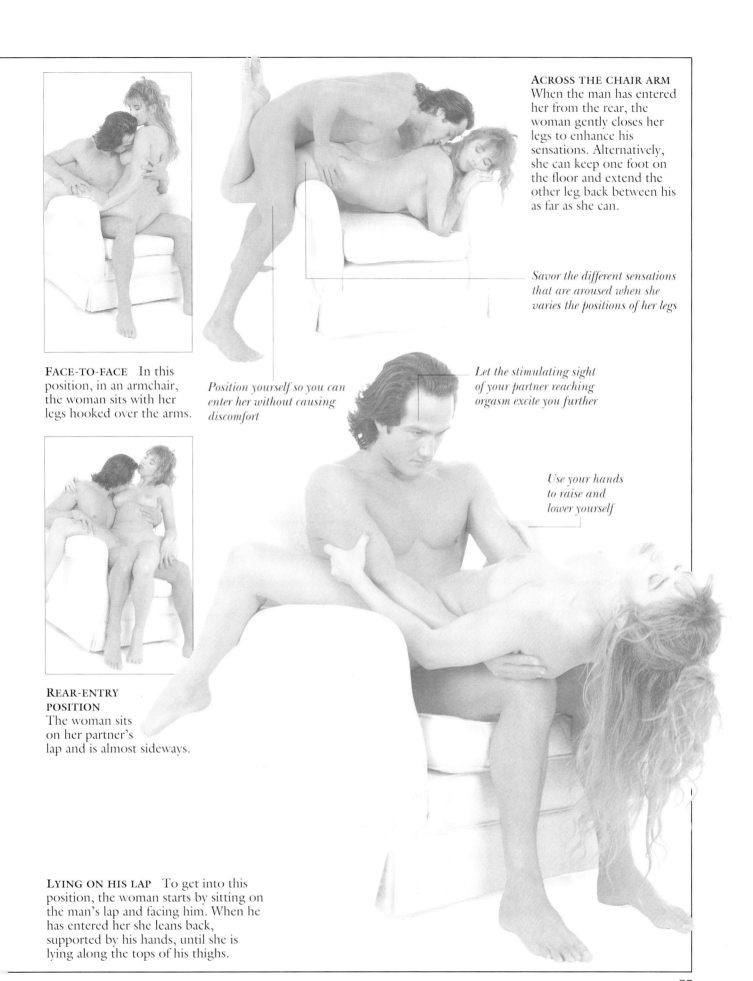

ACROSS THE CHAIR ARM
When the man has entered her from the rear, the woman gently closes her legs to enhance his sensations. Alternatively, she can keep one foot on the floor and extend the other leg back between his as far as she can.

Savor the different sensations that are aroused when she varies the positions of her legs

FACE-TO-FACE In this position, in an armchair, the woman sits with her legs hooked over the arms.

Position yourself so you can enter her without causing discomfort

Let the stimulating sight of your partner reaching orgasm excite you further

Use your hands to raise and lower yourself

REAR-ENTRY POSITION
The woman sits on her partner's lap and is almost sideways.

LYING ON HIS LAP To get into this position, the woman starts by sitting on the man's lap and facing him. When he has entered her she leans back, supported by his hands, until she is lying along the tops of his thighs.

HOW CAN WE RECHARGE OUR SEXUAL BATTERIES?

"After reaching our sexual limits, we must give our bodies time to recover"

THERE IS A famous essay by Viva, the model and celebrity, written in the early 1970s. It is based on her experiment of staying in bed and making love for three days without stopping. On Day Three she complains that she doesn't seem able to come anymore.

What she was describing was an exaggerated version of what would happen to any one of us if we tried to make love constantly. The brain intervenes and enforces rest, to protect the body from death by orgasm.

Some young couples, however, expect their bodies to work like machines, and they view the slowing down of their climaxes with dismay and, in some cases, anxiety. Their dismay is, of course, perfectly understandable, but this kind of slowing down is completely natural and nothing to worry about.

CASE STUDY *Steve & Linda*

Steve and Linda's sexual relationship started off spectacularly, but within a few months it was beginning to cause them problems. Steve found that he couldn't climax as easily and as often as he could before, and Linda had lost interest and was getting bored.

Name:	STEVE
Age:	19
Marital status:	SINGLE
Occupation:	STUDENT

Steve was in his first sexual relationship. He was anxious by nature and slightly greedy, and when he was enthusiastic about something or someone he bordered on the obsessive.

"In the early days of our relationship we made love all the time," he said. "It was wonderful. I came over and over again; it was almost like having multiple orgasms. The first weekend we spent together I had sixteen orgasms. I could hardly move on Monday. And Linda was just as hot as I was. But lately — we've been going together for about seven months now — it hasn't felt so good. She doesn't want to make love so often and complains that it hurts.

"And I can't come as often as I used to before. It's become difficult to climax more than three times. But it feels awfully soon for my body to start running down like this. What's wrong with us?"

Name:	LINDA
Age:	18
Marital status:	SINGLE
Occupation:	STUDENT

Linda, also in her first sexual relationship, was a pale, thin girl. When I spoke to her away from Steve, she showed that she was angry and upset, but in his presence she wrung her hands and was slow to speak.

"Steve just wants sex all the time," she complained. "We never do anything else together except go to bed. And to be quite truthful, I'm getting bored. He never asks me if I want to make love, just plunges on in there. I do like sex, very much, but now it really does hurt me when we have it. That's because I can't get properly interested and so I'm dry. When he spends hours on intercourse it's very painful for me, and also, he takes longer and longer to get to orgasm. The other night he was grinding away for nearly an hour before he managed to come. I was shattered. I don't know how to handle this."

THERAPIST'S ASSESSMENT

Most people, on first discovering sex, want a lot of it and manage more climaxes then than at most other times in their lives. It may be the sheer novelty, or the pent-up sex urge, or simply the fact that most people discover sex when they are young, and young people, particularly young men, have high sex drives.

So teenagers having sex sixteen times in a weekend, at the beginning of their first-ever sexual relationship, may not be so rare. What would be unusual, though, would be if this average were to be maintained. The brain has its natural methods of slowing down the body for its own good. If, for example, sexual pleasure were completely addictive, we might be in danger of climaxing ourselves to death. The brain therefore provides a natural cutoff point, a sort of sexual thermostat which puts an end to climaxes until the body regains its sexual energy.

RECHARGING
It helps, in this instance, to think of the body as a giant sexual battery which, if overloaded, runs out of energy. The simple answer to recharging is to wait awhile and practice abstinence, or at least abstinence from orgasm. Many young people see their body as a machine and can't understand when it refuses to continue automatically with the desired response. But the body possesses a sensitive brain, and sexuality isn't just about the pleasure of orgasm. It's about erotic buildup too.

RECEPTIVENESS
The brain plays a strong part in how receptive you may be to a partner's overtures. If you begin to dislike that partner because of the bull-headed methods they use to go about securing their own pleasure, with no thought for your sensitivity, then not surprisingly you are going to get turned off. Linda, for example, felt she never had any choice in their sex life and that her feelings were stampeded over. If there was any hope for their future together, Steve needed to see Linda as an individual and not as a toy for his pleasure.

EXPLORING SENSUALITY
Together, the young couple decided to explore types of sensuality other than intercourse. They practised sensual massage (pages 56-59) and Taoist methods of lovemaking (page 80) in order to build up a sexual "charge" again. Steve couldn't climax as often as he wanted to, but he could regain the intensity of orgasmic feeling.

My program for
PSYCHIC SEXUAL HEALTH

The idea of "recharging the body's sexual batteries" is not a new one. Thousands of years ago, the ancient Taoists of China perceived the body as possessing an energy flow, and according to their observations this body energy can be both used up and restored. Just as the whole body possesses meridian points, which can be tapped or stimulated by acupuncture in order to restore a healthy balance of energy, so too, the Taoist philosophers argued, do the genitals. Like the feet and hands, the penis and the vagina are thus reflexology zones — areas that, if massaged in the correct way, will stimulate the flow of energy so as to benefit the energy levels elsewhere in the body.

Stage RESTORE ENERGY

Science has so far been unable to verify that acupuncture meridian points exist or to explain why acupuncture works. But acupuncture does work — you need only watch a video of a Chinese patient enduring an operation under the hands of a traditional acupuncturist rather than under anesthesia to see for yourself. The patient feels no pain if the acupuncture is performed correctly.

ENERGY EMISSION In addition to acupuncture's demonstration of energy meridians, Kirlian photography may be used to demonstrate energy emission from the body. Kirlian photography is done with high-voltage equipment that is fast and powerful enough to show, in a photograph of a hand, for example, little shooting darts of energy, like tiny flames, coming from all over it. When a person with lesser energy touches your hand, the brilliance and height of your "flame" diminishes, tapped by the other. It looks as if, simply by contact, energy becomes depleted.

Deer Exercise p82

ENERGY POINTS Sleep, of course, restores energy, but the Taoists say that, as with acupuncture and reflexology, so too do certain sexual practices that evenly stimulate the energy points on the penis and vagina. The Deer Exercise is one way of working toward this. As a result of this type of stimulation, certain glands in the body, which control sexual function, will be placed in an even balance and thus will act in a preventative way, safeguarding sexual health and vigor.

Stage THE SETS OF NINE

Most people are familiar with the theory of Foot Reflexology. Practitioners of this believe that applying stimulation to nerve endings in the foot will stimulate related organs. As previously mentioned, there are similar nerve endings or reflexology zones on the penis and vagina. The Sets of Nine is a Taoist exercise designed to massage these genital reflexology zones evenly and thus to benefit the related organs.

These organs — the Seven Glands — are the pineal, the pituitary, the thyroid, the thymus, the pancreas, the adrenal glands and the sexual glands (prostate and testes in the man and ovaries in the female).

GENITAL MASSAGE Regular and usual intercourse does not evenly massage the penis or the vagina, since the folds of the vaginal canal and the uneven shape of the penis make this difficult. The Sets of Nine — one Set of Nine being a total of ninety strokes — aims to correct this. Many men may find it difficult to go the whole Set of Nine without ejaculating, and Taoist sex instructors encourage their pupils not to lose heart if this happens, saying that even part of the exercise is beneficial to the internal organs and that if lovers continue to practice comfortably, at their own pace, it will become easier to complete one Set of Nine. Serious students should aim at many further sets. The Taoist technique of "injaculation" can be used in conjunction with the Sets of Nine, both for its beneficial effect on the man and for its usefulness in helping him prolong intercourse.

Stage   INJACULATION

All men understand how to ejaculate, but in Taoist sex practice, the man "injaculates." By pressing the Jen-Mo point — an acupressure point on the perineum, halfway between the anus and the scrotum — the ejaculation can, say the Taoists, be reversed and the semen recycled into the bloodstream and reabsorbed. The man still feels pleasurable sensations, and these are, in fact, greatly accentuated since the pressure means that the orgasm happens in very slow spasms. An orgasm may continue for as long as five minutes.

Although he still experiences orgasm, he retains his erection or can regain it quickly, allowing him to continue intercourse far longer. Since he is not expelling his vital substances he will, according to Taoist principles, be preserving energy.

Pressing the Jen-Mo point is easy. Simply reach around behind you at the appropriate moment, and press so that the semen is not allowed to travel out of the prostate and through the urethra. You may like to practice this in private first. The pressure should be neither too firm nor too soft. If you apply pressure too close to the anus, the move won't work. If you press too close to the scrotum, the semen will go into the bladder, rather than the bloodstream, and make your urine cloudy when you urinate. Do not try injaculation if you have a prostate infection.

THE SETS OF NINE The Sets of Nine is a form of sexual intercourse that gives energy-restoring massage to the vagina and penis.

THE SETS OF NINE

To carry out the Sets of Nine, first decide on a comfortable position for intercourse. Then, for each Set of Nine, the man should begin a series of ninety deep and shallow strokes as follows:

1 He thrusts only the penis head into the vagina before withdrawing. He does this shallow stroke nine times, and then he thrusts the entire penis into the vagina once.

2 He follows this up with eight of the shallow strokes (with the penis head only) and two deep strokes (with the entire penis).

3 Next, he makes seven shallow strokes and three deep ones, then ...

4 Six shallow strokes and four deep ones

5 Five shallow strokes and five deep ones

6 Four shallow strokes and six deep ones

7 Three shallow strokes and seven deep ones

8 Two shallow strokes and eight deep ones

9 Finally, he makes one shallow stroke followed by nine deep ones.

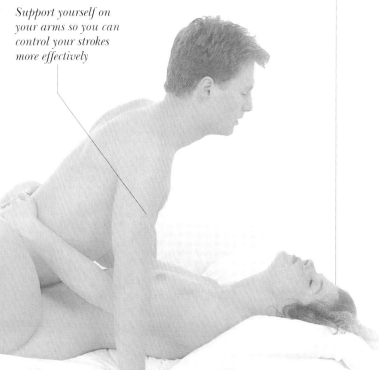

Support yourself on your arms so you can control your strokes more effectively

Combinations of deep and shallow strokes are the key to the Sets of Nine

THE DEER EXERCISE

Over two thousand years ago, in China, Taoist thinkers deduced that the deer, noted for its long life and its strong reproductive activities, exercised its anus when it wiggled its tail. Putting two and two together, they developed a "tail-wiggling" concept for man — which they called the Deer Exercise — designed to rejuvenate him and to create conditions for increasing his sexual arousal. In a similar way, the version of the Deer Exercise for women is said by the Taoists to rebalance the female hormones, encourage sexual energy, and keep a woman looking younger.

WARM HANDS The Deer Exercise involves self-massage, so before you begin, it is a good idea to make sure that your hands are warm, either by rubbing them vigorously together or by washing them in hot water.

You will feel a brief tingling sensation ascend your spinal column, ending somewhere between your ears as you relax

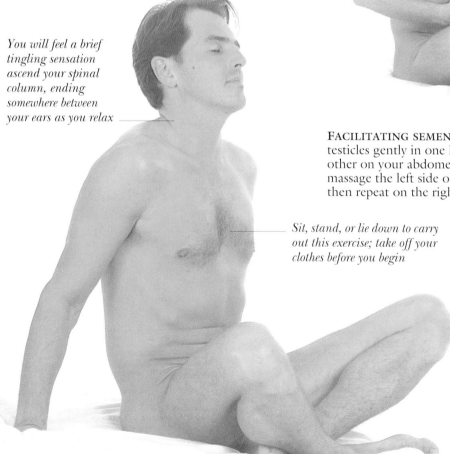

Sit, stand, or lie down to carry out this exercise; take off your clothes before you begin

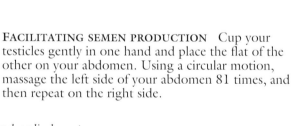

FACILITATING SEMEN PRODUCTION Cup your testicles gently in one hand and place the flat of the other on your abdomen. Using a circular motion, massage the left side of your abdomen 81 times, and then repeat on the right side.

PROSTATE MASSAGE This part of the exercise strengthens the anal muscles, which in turn massage the prostate. Squeeze the anal muscles tightly together and hold as long as you comfortably can. Relax for a minute, then repeat. Do this as many times as you can without discomfort. Taoist teachers say that anal contractions massage the prostate gland, producing hormone secretion and a natural high.

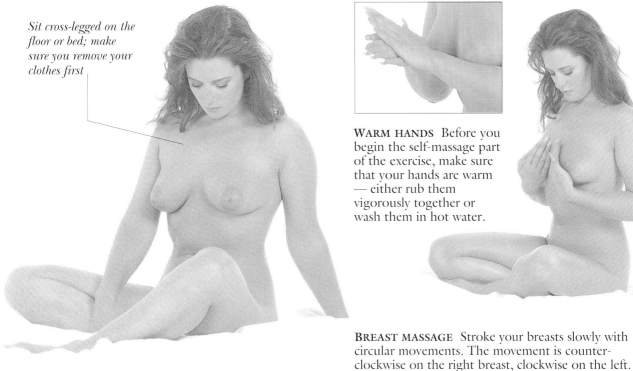

Sit cross-legged on the floor or bed; make sure you remove your clothes first

WARM HANDS Before you begin the self-massage part of the exercise, make sure that your hands are warm — either rub them vigorously together or wash them in hot water.

VAGINAL PRESSURE Sit cross-legged with the heel of one foot pressed up against your vaginal entrance. If this is difficult, place a small ball between your foot and vagina. The pressure from heel or ball stimulates sexual feelings and releases sexual energy.

BREAST MASSAGE Stroke your breasts slowly with circular movements. The movement is counter-clockwise on the right breast, clockwise on the left. Massage your breasts this way at least 36 times and at most 360, in the morning and again in the evening.

DRAWING UP ENERGY Massage each breast in turn with one hand, using the other hand to press your vaginal opening. Contract the muscles in your vagina and anus as if you were trying to control a flow of urine, then focus hard on contracting the anus further. Hold this position for as long as possible, then relax and repeat twenty times. Try to build up the number of times you are able to do this. To check that you are doing it properly, insert a finger into the vagina to see if you can grip it, or at least tighten on it.

Use one hand to stroke your breasts

Contract your vagina and anus correctly to experience a deep and satisfying feeling traveling fleetingly from your anus up through your spine to your ears

Use one hand to press against your vaginal opening

TANTRIC STROKING

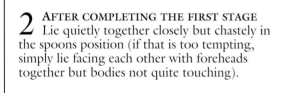

Tantric stroking is an Eastern version of Masters and Johnson's "sensate focus" therapy. But it is a version with a major difference. The first half of the exercise echoes the "touch for pleasure's sake" principle, but the second moves on to something more profound that touches the spirit as well as the body. There are two sensations to be appreciated. The first is your own — what you feel when you touch your partner. The second is what your partner feels when touched by you, and the Tantric lovestroke exercise will teach you how to tune in to that sensation as if it were your own.

After stroking the arms and legs, sit closer and stroke each other's back

Begin by stroking each other's shoulders, arms, and legs

1 BASIC STROKES
Without speaking, lightly stroke each other first with a circling action and then up and down. Avoid the breasts and genitals. Stroke slowly for about 15 minutes, take a break, then repeat the stroking for another 15 minutes. Later in the evening, repeat the stroking for 30 minutes, and imagine that you feel the touch you are giving your partner as if it were you receiving it.

2 AFTER COMPLETING THE FIRST STAGE
Lie quietly together closely but chastely in the spoons position (if that is too tempting, simply lie facing each other with foreheads together but bodies not quite touching).

Enjoy the closeness of your bodies, but do not have intercourse

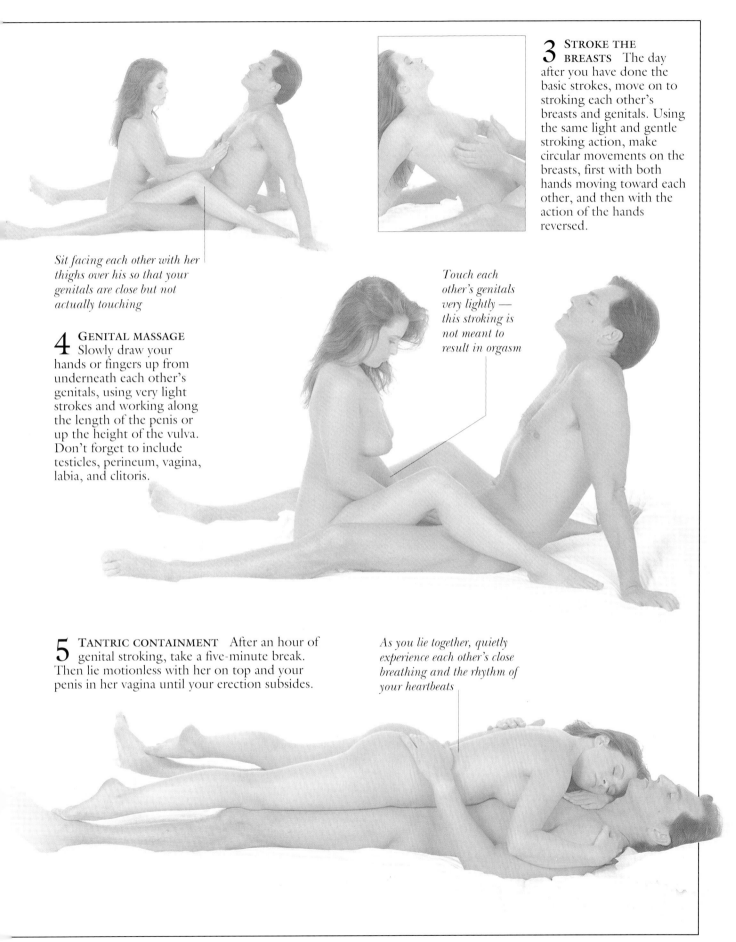

3 STROKE THE BREASTS The day after you have done the basic strokes, move on to stroking each other's breasts and genitals. Using the same light and gentle stroking action, make circular movements on the breasts, first with both hands moving toward each other, and then with the action of the hands reversed.

Sit facing each other with her thighs over his so that your genitals are close but not actually touching

4 GENITAL MASSAGE Slowly draw your hands or fingers up from underneath each other's genitals, using very light strokes and working along the length of the penis or up the height of the vulva. Don't forget to include testicles, perineum, vagina, labia, and clitoris.

Touch each other's genitals very lightly — this stroking is not meant to result in orgasm

5 TANTRIC CONTAINMENT After an hour of genital stroking, take a five-minute break. Then lie motionless with her on top and your penis in her vagina until your erection subsides.

As you lie together, quietly experience each other's close breathing and the rhythm of your heartbeats

TANTRIC INTERCOURSE

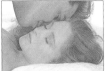

Tantric sex aims to prolong sexual arousal. The stroking described on the previous pages is followed by very slow intercourse. The penis penetrates the vagina by only an inch or so, stays there for a full minute, withdraws and rests in the clitoral hood for a further minute, then slides back in. During subsequent rest minutes the penis first waits on the outside of the vulva for the next strokes, and then eventually waits just inside it.

THE LATERAL POSITION
Prolonged intercourse is facilitated if the couple lies on their sides facing each other. She lies with one leg between his and the other over him.

Lie partly on your back, with your partner lying partly on her front

Pass your lower arm underneath her, pulling her toward you

THE MISSIONARY POSITION
This use of this versatile position is intended to facilitate prolonged intercourse. The advantage of the missionary position is that he can raise himself slightly to one side so that one of his hands can reach back to grasp his testicles and pull them downward should he need to control an impending orgasm.

ORGASM CONTROL
Many men find it easier to reach between their legs to grasp their testicles than to reach around behind to get at them.

Lift your hips slightly while tightening your buttocks

As you near orgasm, prevent it from happening by firmly but gently pulling down on your testicles

To free one hand to grasp your testicles, use the other to raise yourself and support your weight

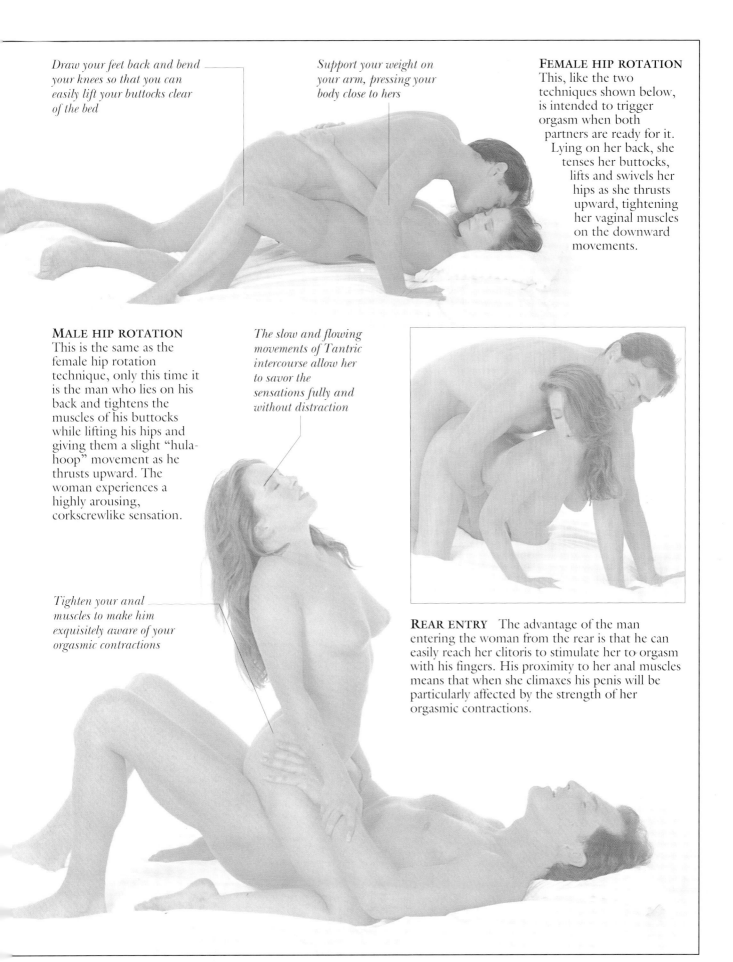

Draw your feet back and bend your knees so that you can easily lift your buttocks clear of the bed

Support your weight on your arm, pressing your body close to hers

FEMALE HIP ROTATION
This, like the two techniques shown below, is intended to trigger orgasm when both partners are ready for it. Lying on her back, she tenses her buttocks, lifts and swivels her hips as she thrusts upward, tightening her vaginal muscles on the downward movements.

MALE HIP ROTATION
This is the same as the female hip rotation technique, only this time it is the man who lies on his back and tightens the muscles of his buttocks while lifting his hips and giving them a slight "hula-hoop" movement as he thrusts upward. The woman experiences a highly arousing, corkscrewlike sensation.

The slow and flowing movements of Tantric intercourse allow her to savor the sensations fully and without distraction

Tighten your anal muscles to make him exquisitely aware of your orgasmic contractions

REAR ENTRY The advantage of the man entering the woman from the rear is that he can easily reach her clitoris to stimulate her to orgasm with his fingers. His proximity to her anal muscles means that when she climaxes his penis will be particularly affected by the strength of her orgasmic contractions.

USING SEX AIDS

"One man was so intrigued by his partner's use of a vibrator to give herself a climax that he learned to use it on her during intercourse so that she came with him inside her."

WE ARE NOT brought up to think of vibrators as natural additions to the act of sex, mainly because these objects are patently artificial. Yet vibrators, used sensitively, provide women with more stimulation than either penis or fingers and act as a catalyst to the elusive orgasm.

Vibrators are especially useful to women who suffer from what is called "automatic switch-off": because of unconscious anxiety during intercourse, their minds are distracted from sex into thinking negative thoughts that prevent climax. They may be able to become very sexually excited and reach a level — which Masters and Johnson aptly called the "plateau phase" — and from there, if they could relax mentally, they could take off into the heights of climax. But sometimes that unconscious anxiety holds them back.

In many such cases, all that the woman needs to overcome this anxiety and have an uninhibited climax is more stimulation, and the use of a vibrator will often provide her with that.

CASE STUDY *Pauline*

Pauline and her husband had an excellent relationship, and they both enjoyed sex. But Pauline rarely climaxed, and she had resorted to faking orgasms so as not to disappoint her partner, Leon, and make him feel inadequate as a lover. This strategy of faking orgasms was effective in that it encouraged Leon's self-confidence and his belief that he was a good lover, but as time went by Pauline began to feel increasingly dissatisfied at her own lack of real orgasms.

Name:	PAULINE
Age:	28
Marital status:	MARRIED
Occupation:	PHYSICAL THERAPIST

Pauline, married to Leon, a welfare officer, was sexily dressed in a low-cut blouse and was very vivacious. She and her husband had been married for three years, had no children, and were very open with each other about sexual matters.

"Leon and I make love often," she told me. "He makes me feel very sexy. But I think I've only come with him twice, and each time the orgasm has been very faint. Leon buys sex manuals and we read them together. I've taught myself to masturbate from them, and I get very turned on by some of the "dirty" stories in them. But although masturbation feels nice, I don't climax from it.

"Leon has been anxious for me to get help with this. He's very supportive. He hasn't had other lovers since we've been together, but he did once help me go to bed with a woman I liked. He took her partner out drinking so that I could go to bed with her. It was very exciting. In fact, we made love on more than one occasion. I still didn't come, though.

"Leon and I are very loving and cuddly with each other. When we're in bed together, sometimes I know I'm near orgasm. But then part of me seems to turn off at that realization. I find it hard to relax because I'm being watched by Leon. That turns me off. I'm frightened Leon is going to be so upset by my not climaxing that in the end we'll split up. I love him a great deal. I don't want that to happen.

"I have to confess that I do fake orgasm with Leon sometimes. I don't do this very often. Maybe one in four or five lovemaking sessions. I don't want him to feel he's not a success in bed. It's important for him to think of himself as a good lover. And quite frequently I feel totally satisfied by him coming. He's had such obvious pleasure from his climax and he's been so loving to me as a result of it, that I've felt a pleasure and satisfaction through him even though I myself don't technically come. But recently that hasn't been enough for me."

THERAPIST'S ASSESSMENT

What Pauline described were several common problems that get in the way of sexual enjoyment for many people. Always feeling that Leon was watching her meant that she had performance fears. When you are focusing on your performance there isn't space left in your brain to focus on heightened sensations. She needed to learn how to cut out her overawareness of Leon and focus instead on herself.

FAKING ORGASM
Faking orgasm may sometimes be expedient for the reasons Pauline outlined. But if you do it too often, it produces not only the negative effect of never allowing you to find out how to climax through intercourse, but it actually teaches your partner the wrong methods of getting you to orgasm.

Naturally, if he thinks a particular method of lovemaking works well for you, he's likely to continue using it, thereby compounding the problem. Having the courage to confess sometimes that things aren't working quite right, and asking for his patience and for different stimulation, is the road to opening up trust — and of course to orgasm. This is where vibrators can help. Sometimes, what is needed in order to get to orgasm is quite simply more stimulation. And a vibrator can provide that when a penis and fingers are flagging. But raising the subject with your partner, and persuading him to let using a vibrator become a regular part of your lovemaking, can often be a difficult move to make.

USING A VIBRATOR
I recommended that Pauline practised self-massage and masturbation over a period of about four weeks, incorporating vibrator use (see page 90) toward the end of that time. I also suggested that she try to become more assertive so that she could work up enough courage to ask Leon if they might include use of the vibrator in their lovemaking (see page 90). Use of the vibrator, plus learning to focus on some especially sexual thoughts and fantasies, helped Pauline overcome her performance fears and reach orgasm.

My program for
INTRODUCING SEX AIDS

The answer to the question "Why use sex aids?" is "Why not?" They are fun to use, and sex should be fun as often as possible. It doesn't always have to be intense or deeply romantic or full of spiritual meaning. Sometimes it can be wonderful when it's just fooling around. And the great advantage of sex aids is that you can use them privately to assist your lighthearted experience of self-pleasuring, as well as using them on an inventive and playful partner.

Sex aids are not a recent invention: they have been around for at least the last 2,500 years. The ancient Egyptians used dildos, and a Greek vase of the fifth century B.C. shows a woman putting one enormous dildo into her mouth while a second one penetrates her vagina. The Romans made candles designed to look like huge penises, and ancient Chinese scripts tell of the custom of binding the base of the penis with silk, a method of retaining erection (an early cock ring).

The Chinese "hedgehog" was a circle of fine feathers, bound onto a silver ring that fitted over the penis. This enabled the lucky woman in question to be tickled to orgasm. Even the idea of a vibrator may have had its origin in the 1800s when female mill workers, leaning against the vibrating handles of the machinery, earned an unexpected bonus.

Sex aid prediction for the future is the sex robot. It will be programmed to overcome any sex problem — you will simply plug yourself into it and the machine will do the rest. (Remember Woody Allen and the 'Orgasmatron' in *Sleeper*?)

Stage 1 FIND OUT WHAT'S AVAILABLE

Perusal of any sex aid catalog (available from sex aid stores or by mail order through advertisements in sex magazines) will show a plethora of dildos, vibrators, cock rings, play balls, fruit-flavored massage oils and, inflatable plastic dolls, and other masturbation aids for both men and women, and usually a selection of harmless bondage items such as silken cords, blindfolds, and handcuffs. These items are relatively inexpensive and, in terms of the endless hours of enjoyment they can provide, they are generally worth the money.

DILDOS AND VIBRATORS There are any number of dildos designed in various shapes and sizes, including the double-headed dildos used by lesbian couples. The vibrator is a modern variation of the dildo and is undoubtedly the most successful sex aid ever invented.

There are vibrators that simply vibrate, and there are multispeed ones that vary in their speed of vibration from slow to supersonic. There are soft rubber ones that twist and undulate, and double ones intended for vagina and anus, with a special attachment for the clitoris, that both twist and vibrate.

There are small, slim anal vibrators with a safeguard across the top to prevent them from disappearing at an inappropriate moment. There are small cigarette-shaped vibrators designed solely for intense clitoral stimulation, and there are pink vibrating eggs which can be inserted into the vagina and switched on as you do housework or type your masterpiece.

COCK RINGS AND PLAY BALLS Cock rings are rings designed to fit closely around the base of the penis, so that the blood flow of erection is trapped inside the penis for as long as possible, should it show signs of leaking away. Play balls, or ben-wa balls, are small weighted balls for women to slip inside their vaginas, where they roll around and produce erotic sensations. The ancient Japanese were the first to use these, and Japanese women would swing in hammocks, enjoying the turn-on.

OILS, DOLLS, AND BONDAGE Fruit-flavored massage oils are specially manufactured to make oral sex tasty, and plastic inflatable dolls are designed for men and women who want to pretend they are making love to a partner when one is not available. There are versions which can be filled with hot water or, at the other end of the scale, there are rubber labia and vaginas which can claim to be "the easiest lay in the world" since they can be carried in a pocket and produced anywhere. The items of bondage equipment speak for themselves.

Despite the variety of aids now on the market, though, a vibrator is probably the best choice for a couple.

Stage 2 CHOOSING A VIBRATOR

There are two principal kinds of vibrator: those that are battery operated and those that run on electricity. The cigar-shaped battery vibrators with varying speeds of vibration are the most convenient. You don't need a great variety of heads to make their stimulation work successfully, but you do need a suitable speed of vibration.

VIBRATOR POWER Research has shown that the optimum vibration speed for facilitating a climax is 80 cycles per second. Some women need such intense stimulation, which is almost impossible to obtain by hand, and this greater frequency of vibration is best obtained on the expensive electric Japanese vibrators.

If you are using a battery-powered vibrator, invest in the long-life alkaline batteries; although these are more expensive than the standard carbon type, they are more powerful and last longer. Vibrator batteries lose power surprisingly quickly, and often, when a woman thinks she has lost the ability to climax when using her vibrator, it turns out that the batteries have run down and so the vibrator is running at well below its usual speed.

Stage 3 USING A VIBRATOR

Vibrators are a useful means of ensuring that some women climax who might otherwise never manage it. But they are also a means of enjoying wonderful clitoral sensation without having to rely on a partner. If there is a partner in your life, it is easy to include use of a vibrator in masturbation and love play and to slip it between your bodies, focused on that strategic point, during intercourse.

Mutual masturbation p46

What many people may not realize is that men also enjoy the sensation of vibration. There are circular vibrators, designed to slip over the penis and rest at the base, capable of bringing the man to climax too.

VIBRATORS AND LOVEMAKING Try using a warmed-up vibrator on each other's body during lovemaking. Take turns running it over each other's shoulders, neck, chest, and breasts, down the sides of the body, and around the abdomen and buttocks. Dart it in and out of the inner thighs, which for most people are sensitive erogenous zones. Explore and probe the vagina with it, and press it very gently in among the folds of the testicles and then around the base of the penis.

INTENSE SENSATIONS The areas that produce the most intense sensations when stimulated by a vibrator are the clitoris and the frenulum of the penis. The rim of the anus, for both men and women, is another good spot to stimulate, and many men get great pleasure from stimulation of the prostate, inside the anus.

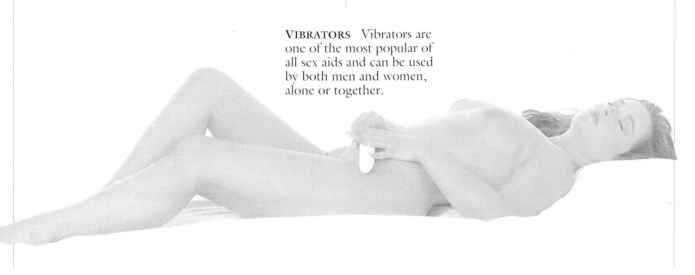

VIBRATORS Vibrators are one of the most popular of all sex aids and can be used by both men and women, alone or together.

HIS SEX ORGANS

In terms of love play and sexual intercourse, the most important single part of a man's genitals is undoubtedly his penis. However, the common belief that a man's virility and his effectiveness as a sexual partner depend on the size of his erect penis is totally misguided — what really counts is the skill and consideration with which he makes love to his partner.

MALE GENITALS The male genitals or sex organs are partly external and partly internal. The external organs are the penis and the scrotum (which contains the testicles, epididymes, and vas deferens), and the internal organs include the prostate gland and the seminal vesicles. During erection, an intricate network of vessels within the penis fills with blood, causing it to swell and stiffen. The urethra, a tube running right through the length of the penis, discharges urine from the bladder and also carries the seminal fluid during ejaculation.

GLANS The glans, the head of the penis, is rich in nerve endings which make it very sensitive to touch.

FRENULUM The highly sensitive frenulum is a small fold of skin between the glans and the shaft.

SHAFT The ridge along the underside of the penis shaft is often very sensitive to touch and stroking.

VAS DEFERENS Each vas deferens (there are two) carries sperm from the epididymis to the seminal vesicle ducts, where it is mixed with seminal fluid for ejaculation.

SEMINAL VESICLE The two seminal vesicles (one on each side of the bladder) produce most of the seminal fluid discharged during ejaculation.

Anus

PROSTATE GLAND Within the prostate gland, which is situated below the neck of the bladder, ducts from the seminal vesicles join the urethra. Manual stimulation of the gland creates intense arousal.

Bladder

Pubic bone

Penis

Urethra

Glans

Foreskin

Epididymis

TESTICLES The testicles (or testes) produce sperm and the male sex hormone testosterone. Sperm, after production, is stored in the epididymes, two long, extensively coiled ducts.

SCROTUM The scrotum has two parts. Each contains one of the testicles, suspended by a spermatic cord containing the vas deferens, blood vessels, and nerves.

HER SEX ORGANS

The external parts of a woman's genitals, and the area immediately surrounding them, are highly sensitive to physical stimulation. This sensitive region extends from the mons pubis (or mound of Venus), the padding of fatty tissue beneath the pubic hair that acts as a sort of cushion during intercourse, back to the perineum, the area between the vulva and the anus.

FEMALE GENITALS Although the female genitals are partly external, most of the organs are hidden away inside the body. The external organs (the vulva or pudendum) include the clitoris, two pairs of skin folds called the labia, and the openings of the vagina and urethra. The complex internal organs include the ovaries, fallopian tubes, uterus, cervix, and vagina. The fallopian tubes connect the ovaries to the uterus or womb, and the cervix connects the uterus to the vagina, into which the man's penis is placed during sexual intercourse.

CLITORIS The abundant nerve endings of the clitoris make it extremely sensitive to stimulation, and when stimulated it swells and becomes even more sensitive.

LABIA MAJORA The outer, larger pair of lips or skin folds that protect the openings of the vagina and urethra are the labia majora.

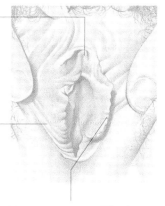

LABIA MINORA The inner labia, the labia minora, secrete a substance called sebum that helps to lubricate the vagina, and they meet at the top to form the hood of the clitoris.

OVARIES The two ovaries each produce eggs, the female hormones estrogen and progesterone, and small amounts of testosterone.

UTERUS After an egg has been fertilized, it moves down into the uterus or womb where it eventually develops into a fetus.

FALLOPIAN TUBES The fallopian tubes transport the eggs from the ovaries and the fertilization of eggs by sperm takes place within them.

Cervix

Bladder

Pubic bone

Urethra

Clitoris

Anus

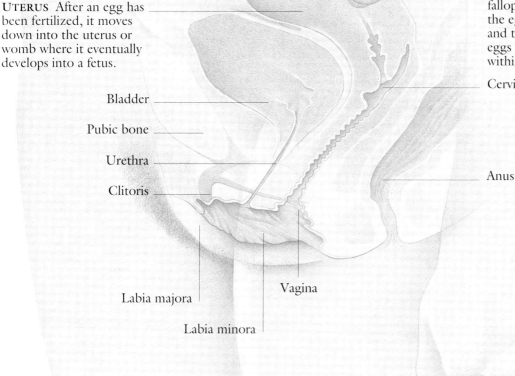

Labia majora

Vagina

Labia minora

INDEX

CARROLL & BROWN
LIMITED would like to thank
Bruce Garrett and Madeline
Weston for their editorial
assistance; Tim Kent and Tula
Whitlow for their photography
assistance; and all the models for
the enthusiasm, co-operation and
professionalism they displayed in
helping us to produce this book.

*ANNE HOOPER'S
INTIMATE SEX GUIDE*
Typesetting: Debbie Rhodes
Film outputting: DTP
Production: Lorraine Baird